Next Geopolitics
The Future of World Affairs
(Technology*)*

Volume One

by

Abishur Prakash

To my mother, father and brother, for their
guidance and patience all these years.

LIFE DISCLAIMER

This book has a finite lifespan. The rate at which technology is advancing and the number of new developments taking place mean that within a short time, **this book will be irrelevant.**

About Me

Before we begin, I'd like to introduce myself. I'm a 25-year-old millennial, living in Canada. Born in New Zealand to Indian parents, I spent my childhood in Australia and grew up in Canada. I've spent time in India and the United States.

It's no surprise then that I've always had a global outlook, and with it, a continual itch to understand the way the world works, and why. My current passion and interest in geopolitics began in 2013, when I took a break from pursuing my university degree and jumped into a project that quite literally re-educated me and introduced me to geopolitics and its concepts.[1]

After that project, I managed to recruit one of the highest-valued startups in the world. For nearly 14 months, I provided the company with actionable intelligence on how its markets around the world were changing. At the same time, I built a network of Fortune 500 executives and CEOs, providing them with geopolitical insights on a weekly basis.

As I moved through these experiences, one constant red flag flashed on my radar. The definition of geopolitics wasn't changing. There appeared to be no real, disruptive attempts to push the envelope and explore what else would make up the geopolitical landscape in the future — at least not in the public domain.

Until now, geopolitics has been defined by variables like oil, natural gas, defense exports, and war. These variables occupy the minds of most geopolitical pundits. Because these are the same pundits from whom companies and governments seek insight, this definition of geopolitics has become the norm.

My itch returned. Was this the only way to define geopolitics? What else will comprise our geopolitical landscape today and tomorrow?

As I searched, I came across several new areas I believe will define the future geopolitical landscape, the most powerful of them being new technologies. One of my first steps in leading this discussion was the article I wrote for *Forbes*.[2] It explored the geopolitical consequences of the South Korean government contracting Samsung to develop robots to replace Chinese labor. How would China respond? I proposed that China could introduce a robot tax for every South Korean import manufactured by robots instead of by Chinese labor.

The pages that follow are my analysis and distillation of how new technologies will change the global geopolitical landscape. It's part of a new era in geopolitics I call "Next Geopolitics."

Regardless of who you are, I hope you have one of two reactions after reading this book: either you completely disagree with me, or you're completely blown away.

Either way, I'd love it if you'd let me know how you found my book. My email is abishur@nextgeopolitics.com.

Abishur Prakash

Key Concepts and Technologies

For those who wish to use this book for educational purposes, below is a list of the key concepts and technologies discussed in the following chapters. They're useful as a primer to introduce people to the geopolitics of technology and the next wave of technologies heading our way.

Concepts

Embryonic Geopolitics: Designer babies are embryos that are edited to have certain traits. They'll create a unique challenge for governments. In the past, if a child was born in the United Kingdom, he or she became a British citizen, with full rights and benefits. Tomorrow, if the child is designed in the United Kingdom but born in India, to which country does the baby belong? And who takes responsibility for the baby in regard to healthcare, tax payments, etc.?

Space Sovereignty: On Earth, countries have operated alongside one another for centuries, yet still confusion, debate, and war exist over territory and borders. In space, where no rules are established and where countries are just beginning to move into establishing space colonies, who sets the rules? More importantly, who has the right to do so?

Food Cloning: In the future, countries will be able to clone goods they once imported from abroad, like plants and meat. Once this takes place, it'll create challenges for free trade. For example, China can clone cows domestically instead of importing beef from India. What will India do to compete with Chinese cloned beef? As more countries pursue food cloning, how will this affect relations between countries?

Dangerous Automation: Automation — the use of machines or software to perform tasks previously conducted by humans — will create social problems for countries. How will governments deal with millions of jobs being automated? One solution is to introduce universal basic income programs or automation quotas (eg, only 25 percent of jobs can go to machines). Each of these strategies, however, come with their own risks.

New Rules of War: In the past, it was clear what constituted an act of war. Going forward, this clarity will disappear as countries and people change the ways they attack and hurt other countries. One way this is already happening is through cyber attacks and cyber warfare. Does a cyber attack on Iran, conducted by Saudi Arabia, constitute an act of war? Should it?

Technological Terrorism: New technologies like self-driving cars, connected appliances, and drones present new opportunities for terrorists to conduct attacks by hijacking these devices. One possible scenario is having terrorists hijack self-driving cars, driving them into parks and onto sidewalks to run over people.

Drone Dependency: Drones are being utilized by countries in a variety of ways. For some countries, they're being used to leapfrog deficits like a lack of roads and highways. The problem, however, is that if these drones stop working tomorrow and people stop receiving the supplies the drones deliver, how will populations react — especially if no roads or highways have been built to provide an alternative delivery method?

Predictive Foreign Policy: Artificial intelligence will give governments capabilities they didn't possess before. One of them is the ability to predict what another country will do. In the future, Russia may be able to predict a Chinese invasion before it takes place. How will this predictive capacity affect the decisions countries make?

Technologies

Artificial Intelligence: the ability of a platform to gain a level of consciousness whereby it can make decisions and choices without human input, and evolve independently

Automation: machines and software executing tasks previously done only by humans

Big Data: distilling huge amounts of data to see new insights, patterns, and trends

Cloning: duplicating a person or object (eg, plant, animal) in a lab, through asexual means

Drones: unmanned robotic machines that can operate and function in various environments

Embryo: a fertilized egg in the process of developing into a baby

Genome: the complete set of information on the structure of an organism, found in a cell

Internet of Things (IoT): the web of devices connected to the Internet

Space Mining: the ability of countries to use advanced machinery and propulsion capabilities to mine objects, such as asteroids, for resources.

Meet the Historian

Imagine it's the year 2050 and you're 20 years old.

It's a quiet Wednesday night, and you're sitting in your living room wearing your virtual reality device. You trekked the Himalayas with a friend for the past two hours, and before that, you explored craters on Mars. Now you're looking for something different to do.

You're at the home screen of the virtual reality system, scanning the different apps. Using your mind, you move through the apps, browsing different genres until you find an app you haven't tried before. It's called "Virtual Historian."

You click on the app, and the surroundings immediately change. Now you're in a library where a virtual historian greets you. "Ask me any question about history and I will answer it," the historian says. A few minutes go by. You walk through the virtual library touching books, reading titles. You want to ask a challenging question.

In a few more minutes, a question pops into your mind. It's based on a documentary you watched the night before about a device that existed at the beginning of the 21st century, called a smartphone. "I can't believe people actually used that thing," you think to yourself.

You turn to the historian and ask, "What technologies have changed the world since the start of the 21st century?"

What do you think this virtual historian, with access to all the data in the world, would say to you?

Likely, the virtual historian's explanation would include many technologies that emerged at different times throughout the past fifty years.

Perhaps the historian would start with Hermes, Professor, Thing, and Fester. These are the first four robots ever used in ground combat, deployed by the U.S. military in Qiqay, Afghanistan, in 2002.[3] Their use signaled the beginning of a new era of coexistence between humans and robots.

Next, the virtual historian might examine the advancements around computing. The historian might say the Apple iPhone 5, a smartphone released in 2012, had 2.7 times the processing power of the Cray-2, a supercomputer from 1985 — or, that the Nintendo Entertainment System (NES), a gaming platform from 1985, had half the processing power of the computer system that was on the Apollo moon missions.[4]

Having touched on the iPhone, the historian might speak about the effects that smartphones had on countries. It could touch on the Umbrella Movement, a pro-democracy movement that took place in Hong Kong in 2014, fueled by a smartphone app called FireChat that allowed protestors to communicate without an Internet connection.[5] The historian might then jump to the impact social media had on the world, fueling revolts against the government like those seen during the Arab Spring in 2011.

The historian goes on.

After passing the 2016 mark, what technologies do you think the historian will talk about? What do you think their impact on the world will be? Will it be artificial intelligence? Autonomous robots (also called "killer robots")? Designer babies? Space exploration and colonization? Food cloning? Or something else entirely?

These technologies and others are part of a tsunami of change approaching the world. In fact, as you'll see, some technologies have already arrived.

All these technologies extend beyond their domains and have far-reaching implications for the way world affairs operate, and the way countries behave with one another. These new technologies will disrupt governments, shift global power, and throw into question the relevance of institutions.

In other words, they will transform the world.

For some people, new technologies are just that — transformative. For others, new technologies are nothing new. Technology has always arrived in transformative waves, and the world hasn't changed that much.

Regardless of what side of the fence you sit on, one thing makes this tsunami of technological change different from those before it. Many of the technologies in this wave have never existed before, in neither their current nor future capacities. As such, they're an entirely new phenomenon with which countries will have to contend.

Some of these technologies, like artificial intelligence or drones, are already advancing. Others, like designer babies and food cloning, are still in their infancy. Regardless of their stage in development, they're all worth our attention.

This book lays out eight scenarios about the implications new technologies will have for our global geopolitical landscape — with each scenario focusing on a different technology.

In the first chapter, we explore the geopolitical implications of designer babies, where science enables parents to edit certain traits of their baby, such as a genetic predisposition to certain diseases.

The second chapter outlines how countries pursuing advances in space, such as space mining and establishing bases on planets, will cause new uncertainty over who calls the shots.

The third chapter dives into automation and the disruption the "Next Machine Age"[6] will bring to countries around the world — even if they're currently investing in strategies to deal with it, such as universal basic income programs.

The fourth chapter looks at the challenges food cloning — the ability of countries to clone goods they once imported — will create for world trade, specifically free trade.

The fifth chapter examines how new technologies, like cyber attacks and autonomous robots, will redefine interactions between countries.

The sixth chapter looks at how drones, smart appliances, and other technologies will provide terrorists with new tools, creating even more security challenges for governments.

The seventh chapter paints a picture of how countries utilizing technologies like drones could be a recipe for disaster.

The eight and final chapter focuses on how artificial intelligence will provide governments with new capabilities to understand where the world is heading.

These scenarios may appear strange, but bear in mind the frequency and kind of change taking place in the world. Nothing is following established models or rules. At the end of the day, the impact of these new technologies on the global geopolitical landscape will be defined by people — including yourself. Therefore, it can only help if you take the time to understand these new technologies and their geopolitical impact, so you can prepare for what is to come.

Chapter 1

Embryonic Geopolitics
Who owns your child?

London, United Kingdom
2025

In January 2025, the United Kingdom passes laws to legalize the commercial sale of designer baby services. From now on, hospitals, clinics, and other registered offices can offer embryo editing to parents for a fixed price. Parents using this service can select certain traits of their child — which will expand as the technology advances — such as skin color, height, and disease vulnerability.

Fueled by a desire to have the baby of their dreams, a couple from Mumbai, India, travels to London in February 2025, and purchases a designer baby service. The process takes two weeks. Once complete, the couple returns to India. Nine months later, in mid-November, the woman gives birth to a healthy baby girl.

Once the birth is complete, the new parents face a new challenge.

Who will bear responsibility for the baby — the country where the baby was designed (the United Kingdom) or the country where the baby was born (India)?

Introduction

You hear of people having children all the time — a friend from college whom you haven't seen in years, a brother or sister who surprised you with a phone call, a former business colleague who finally got married. Regardless of who it is, when you hear that someone is pregnant or expecting, your first thought isn't to start analyzing where this child will be born. Why?

Where a child is born has huge implications. It decides many things for the child before he or she even arrives. It also has a huge impact on the way countries function. Yet so many of us overlook this.

Think about where you were born. It decided whether you had free access to healthcare or paid for it. It decided whether your education was covered by the government or was paid for from your own pocket. It decided how high or low of a tax rate you pay or will pay. It decided how well you'll be taken care of if you need help from the government. It may also have decided if you changed countries.

All these areas, which had a huge impact on the kind of life you've lived, were not determined by how high your GPA was, how good looking you were (or still are), or the kind of friendships you kept or lost. It was all based on where you were born — a stroke of luck or misfortune.

This is just one side of the coin. Think about your birth from the government's point of view. You represent a cost and revenue source. You're a cost because you cost money to maintain — education, healthcare, emergency services, social services, etc. You're a revenue source because you make money for the government — income tax, property tax, goods and services tax, unemployment payments, pension payments, etc.

This is the basic model that has guided people and countries for the past millennia. A baby costs X, Y, Z. The baby will eventually pay X, Y, Z. In the future, this model is at risk of breaking down because of a technology called embryo editing. Soon, you'll be asking your friend, sibling or colleague not only when and where the baby will be born, but how it was conceived. That could be an awkward conversation.

What is embryo editing? Before we can define that, we have to define an embryo. When a male sperm enters the egg of a female, it creates what's known as a zygote. This zygote, after traveling through part of the body, evolves and divides into a blastocyst. This blastocyst has two components. The inner part is the embryo, which eventually becomes the baby. The outer part is the membrane, which protects the embryo.[7] The embryo itself only exists for eight to ten weeks from the date of fertilization, at which point the embryo turns into a fetus.[8]

Science has now reached a point where it can edit certain features of the baby while it's in the embryonic phase — between fertilization and fetus. This editing takes place in the genome within the embryo (the genome contains the DNA).[9] This process of editing the embryo is known as embryo editing.

Features of the baby that can be edited include resistance to diseases, such as a blood disorder, and potentially in the future, more advanced features like skin color, intelligence, and more. These kinds of future babies are often called designer babies.

This is where the entire model that has guided childbirth and government responsibility is at risk of breaking down. To whom do these designer babies belong? Who pays for them? Equally important — who protects them?

Whose Baby? Whose Responsibility?

The United Kingdom is one of a handful of countries leading the first advances when it comes to embryo editing. In February 2016, the UK-based Francis Crick Institute received approval to begin editing in vitro fertilization embryos. Scientists there work with a fertilized egg during the first seven days of development.[10] Their objective is to alter genes in the embryo shortly after fertilization to find solutions to infertility. After seven days, the embryos are destroyed.[11]

This approval comes as the United Kingdom tries to tap every sector of its economy — including those that aren't fully regulated or legal. In late 2014, the United Kingdom overtook France as the world's fifth largest economy, after adding prostitution and drugs to its GDP.[12]

In the future, could the United Kingdom become a hub for designer babies, exporting these babies to the world in pursuit of economic growth by overlooking the legalities?

Using the scenario from the beginning of the chapter — where a couple from India travels to the United Kingdom to design their child, returns home, and nine months later has the child in India — a new, complex, cross-border challenge emerges.

To which country does the baby belong — the United Kingdom, where the baby was designed, or India, where the baby was born?

This is a fundamental challenge that faces those governments providing designer babies. Will they claim responsibility for the child they're designing, and if so, what will this responsibility look like?

One of the advantages of being born in the United Kingdom is access to the National Health Service (NHS). It's public healthcare for citizens. Noncitizens from outside the country who access the NHS can be charged for care.[13]

A child designed in the United Kingdom can demand access to free healthcare even though he or she is born outside the country. The United Kingdom may be inclined to reject such requests, as it could become expensive. But if the United Kingdom refuses to pay for the healthcare of the designer baby, it automatically puts the onus of responsibility on India.

India may refuse to pay for the child's healthcare. Instead, it may demand that the United Kingdom and India split the costs, as the child originated from both countries. Or India may refuse to pay at all, and shift the onus back onto the United Kingdom. London and New Delhi could find themselves in a pointing match over who takes care of these designer babies. During all this, the designer baby itself is caught in the middle.

Who can delegate such an issue? Institutions like the United Nations (UN), World Trade Organization (WTO), World Health

Organization (WHO), and others were not created with these new technologies in mind. Designer babies are an entirely new phenomenon for these institutions. What will their role be, if any?

In the past, when it has come to issues such as territorial disputes, institutions have taken a black-and-white approach. For example, the Philippines filed a case in 2013 with the Permanent Court of Arbitration (PCA) against China over the South China Sea. In mid-2016, the court ruled against China's claim to the region.[14] This is a traditional black-and-white approach, with a ruling in favor of the Philippines and against China.

This same black-and-white approach won't work when it comes to designer babies, because they represent a fundamental change in the way children are born. Before, children originated from one country. Now, they may originate from two.

Things become even more complicated when countries want to reject certain responsibilities but claim benefits. Healthcare is an expenditure; therefore, countries will not want to accept that responsibility. Another expenditure similar to healthcare is free education, and depending on the country, can include college and university.[15] While healthcare and education represent costs, taxes are a revenue source — a benefit of having a child born in a given country. A child originating from two countries will raise questions over which can claim the taxes. Are both countries entitled to the taxes the child will pay when he or she grows up?

If India, in fact, evaded responsibility and the United Kingdom pays for the child's healthcare, can India come back later and claim a percentage of the taxes? What if the United Kingdom and India had split the costs — will they split the taxes?

These are all grey areas. Designer babies will jolt countries into action and this means, initially, that each country will be designing its own separate policies that match its needs and challenges.

Designer Baby Havens

Today, the world is trying to crack down on tax havens like the Bahamas, Switzerland, or the British Virgin Islands. These countries' extremely low tax rates allow companies and people to park their money and have no fear of losing any of it. In the future, will countries pursue becoming designer baby havens through policy? If so, why?

Many countries will want to avoid responsibility for designer babies. Each will have its own reasons. Designer babies may present problems for the economy, society (including religions), global image, and more. But a small set of countries may welcome designer babies because they solve various problems. Two countries that fall into the latter category are China and Japan. This is because the populations of China and Japan are rapidly aging.

By 2050, for every 100 people in China aged twenty to sixty-four, forty-five people will be over sixty-five years old — more than 25 percent of the entire population.[16] China's aging population is viewed as the main reason for the government lifting its one-child policy in 2015. This is not expected to have any real effect for the next 20 years, however.[17]

In Japan, the median age of farmers is now sixty-seven.[18] In February 2016, new data showed the Japanese population had contracted by almost one million in five years.[19] At the same time, 25 percent of all citizens are now over the age of sixty-five,[20] and the Japanese population is expected to shrink by one-third by 2060.[21]

For China and Japan, designer babies present a new way to grow the population. Either country can introduce policies that cover 100 percent of a designer baby's expenses for life — including healthcare, education, unemployment insurance, and more — as long as the designer baby lives in the country and creates a family.

This puts aside any confusion or debate over which country pays for what. It does not, however, settle the debate over which country can claim what — that will remain a challenge. Perhaps China and Japan can also introduce a policy to claim a percentage of the revenue that designer babies generate over their lifetimes while living in the country.

In essence, China and Japan could become havens for designer babies, if they ensure that these babies will face no difficulties and are protected and taken care of — even if other countries neglect those responsibilities. Such havens are even more likely if the country offering the haven is designing the babies.

China surprised the world in 2015 by announcing that scientists working at Sun Yat-sen University had altered the gene responsible for beta-thalassemia, a deadly blood disorder.[22] It was the first time scientists had edited the human embryo. One year later, in April 2016, Chinese scientists again edited an embryo in an attempt to make it resistant to HIV.[23]

If China becomes a leader in embryo editing, will it neglect its responsibility to take care of these designer babies, or will China use this new soft power to plant the seeds for future population growth?

Designer Baby Trade

When it comes to designer babies, another area of confusion will involve trade rules. In May 2016, the Dutch government approved growing embryos for research.[24] Tomorrow, the Netherlands could approve embryo editing trials and eventually, like the United Kingdom, become a designer baby exporter. If in the future, the Netherlands sells designer babies to other countries, these babies will be considered a Dutch export. What will this mean for trade, especially if institutions like the European Union (EU) introduce rules that make the designer baby trade illegal?

Will the Netherlands or other countries listen, especially if it means letting go of a new growth industry for their economy?

If the Netherlands complies with an EU-ruling that bans the designer baby trade, it will give other countries providing the same services — such as the United Kingdom or China — a greater market share. It could also fuel a new sector of the black market in countries that banned designer babies.

What makes designer babies a real challenge for the European Union and other trade-related institutions is that for the first time in history, trade policies will legalize or ban the trade of new humans. People themselves will become a component of trade rules, and not in terms of trafficking or organ trade (the artificial organ trade presents its own challenges for geopolitics).

When it comes to the designer baby trade, one of the main challenges is that global institutions that facilitate world trade are made up of countries with distinct and unique political systems and social designs.

For example, Malaysia is a member of the Association of Southeast Asian Nations (ASEAN) Economic Community (AEC), an economic zone that launched at the beginning of 2016 for members of the ASEAN. The design of Malaysia is such that religion has an enormous influence. There is little separation between "church and state," or in Malaysia's case, "mosque and state." For Malaysia and other countries where religion remains a dominant force in politics, designer babies may appear blasphemous. Malaysia may therefore choose to ban designer babies.

If the AEC rules that the designer baby trade is legal and Malaysia introduces a ban or tariff on designer babies, the rumblings of a new trade dispute arise. Unlike the past, when trade disputes were over a local industry being crippled by the dumping of foreign imports or exports from another country, this new trade dispute will revolve around religion and governance clashing with globalization.

Another possibility is that world trade will become polarized.

In 2015, China launched a rival to the World Bank and International Monetary Fund, called the Asian Infrastructure Investment Bank (AIIB). The AIIB has Chinese rules and policies, and revolves around an agenda set by Beijing. In the future, China may decide to launch its own trade bloc, such as the Chinese Trade Organization (CTO). Obviously, the CTO would have its own Chinese-centric policies — one possibly being the legal trade of designer babies.

In one scenario, the AEC could legalize the designer baby trade. In another scenario, it could ban this trade. If the AEC rules that the designer baby trade is illegal while the CTO rules that it's legal, then world trade as we know it will come to an end.

A country like Malaysia — which is a founding member of the AEC, but its economic lifeline is China — will likely be a member of both the AEC and the CTO. How would Malaysia comply with the designer baby trade if these two institutions had different policies? This could lead to different trade blocs competing with one another. It could also fracture relationships between countries. Could Malaysia and ASEAN, or Malaysia and China, remain partners if they're on opposite ends of something as controversial as designer babies?

Discrimination Against Designer Babies

Today, the advances around embryo editing and designer babies have to do with editing diseases, as we've seen in the advancements from China. Tomorrow, the editing may also include customizing traits of the child, such as height, skin color, intelligence, and more. Power that was once out of reach could soon be accessed by parents around the world. In addition, this new breed of children, designed to be superior, presents an unprecedented challenge for societies around the world. How will ordinary people, such as you and I, react?

One parent may want a genius, while the other desires a hulk. In either case, whether in education or sports, competitive challenges will emerge for the rest of the population, along with religious and moral challenges. This could lead to discrimination against designer babies. Companies may not hire them to avoid upsetting the rest of the workforce. Violence against them may erupt if ordinary people take out their fear and anger on the adult versions of these designer babies.

In the past, when citizens of a country faced discrimination, it led to civil rights movements and political tension. Will this emerge from discrimination against designer babies? Will countries see the emergence of designer baby work unions, political parties, and institutions, designed to ensure that this new segment of the world's population is protected?

Conclusion

Designer babies have the potential to become as important as currency or energy. This is why the future of embryonic geopolitics will take the world to a crossroads. Countries will have to choose. Do they remain on the path of tradition, grounded in religion, ethics, and history? Or do they move forward into a future driven by technology, advances in science, and new industries?

There is no right or wrong response, but the responses will influence world affairs going forward. Countries that export designer babies will have to grapple with the financial, political, and social obligations of taking care of these people. Designer baby exports will clash with rules set by trade blocs and international institutions. In turn, these rules have the potential to fuel new trade agreements and challenge the relevance of certain institutions.

For some countries, the choice is simple: Designer babies present an economic or demographic opportunity. For others, designer babies represent a combination of opportunity and blasphemy. The wave of designer babies is upon us and unless countries begin defining their positions and policies, world affairs and geopolitics will be disrupted.

Chapter 2

Space Sovereignty
Who controls space?

Asteroid 4B379
March 2036

A warning light goes off on "Zhongguo 1," an asteroid miner China has deployed on "Asteroid 4B379." The asteroid is 30,000 miles from Earth. The warning light indicates that the miner is damaged and unable to move its load to a nearby depository. On Earth, engineers and artificial intelligence in Beijing scan activity feeds and logs to find the source of the damage. An hour later, they identify what caused the damage: external debris.

On Asteroid 4B379, China isn't the only country with a mining operation. The United States, Japan, and France all have their own operations there. Only the Americans, however, are mining in the same area as the Chinese.

Using "Wenjin," China's most advanced satellite, the engineers in Beijing begin to monitor the American mining machine and track the trajectory of the debris flying outward from this machine as its drill pulls gold from the asteroid. After thirty minutes of analysis, they determine that this is the source of the external debris impacting the Chinese miner.

The engineers report this. The Chinese President and his senior staff are briefed. China's prized robotic miner has been damaged and is unable to function. It will take at least six months to send a repair robot or a replacement miner. By then, the asteroid will be too far to mine. And so will the $3 trillion worth of gold it's carrying.

All because of the United States.

Introduction

Think of the map of the world as it exists today. Why does it look the way it does?

For thousands of years, humans have been fighting over territory on Earth. Over time, borders and cultures were shaped and divided. As borders were defined, countries began taking advantage of what lay within or near their borders.

In North America, the United States and Canada control and access the Great Lakes, the largest freshwater system on the planet.[25] In the Middle East, Saudi Arabia controls the largest land mass in the Arabian Peninsula. Within this land mass are huge amounts of oil, putting Saudi Arabia in control of the world's third largest oil reserves after the United States and Russia.[26]

These territories, borders, and resources have guided world affairs for thousands of years. The map we know today is a type of structure under which the world operates.

Now, many countries are looking to expand beyond Earth. The map that has guided them for years is now obsolete. In space, there's only a blank canvas, and every country will try to draw on it.

This isn't the first time countries have ventured into space. The final frontier was a major theme of the Cold War, locking the United States and Soviet Union into a new kind of rivalry beyond arms and ideology. Each side had its accomplishments. In 1957, the Soviet Union launched the world's first satellite, called Sputnik 1. In 1969, the United States became the first country in the world to send humans to the Moon.

Now, decades after the Cold War, several countries are returning to space with a new appetite. This new space race is much different, as more than two powers are involved. The goals and ambitions are far greater than they've ever been before. Countries are operating largely independently, using their own technology and capabilities.

As the world moves toward a new kind of space age, beyond telecommunications and human orbits, there is no map to guide it. Who decides who controls which territory in space? Who determines the rules? Will what happens in space affect what happens on Earth?

Lack of Policy

In 1967, the U.N.'s "Outer Space Treaty" came into effect. Created during the Cold War, it provided a set of rules for conduct in space.[27] When this treaty was created, the world was a different place. Most of the world looked up to the United States. The Soviet Union was the only other global power. Countries like China and India were poor and underdeveloped.

Fast forward to today. Depending on who you ask, by 2030 China will have overtaken the United States as the largest economy in the world. The Soviet Union no longer exists, but Russia is in a period of resurgence, expanding its influence in Eastern Europe, the Middle East, and Asia. Countries like India, Nigeria, and others are fast becoming the most important economies of tomorrow. As economic and geopolitical power shifts, to whom will countries listen as they expand into space?

China is one of the leaders of this new space race. By 2018, China has plans to send a probe to the dark side of the Moon, an unexplored section.[28] If it's successful, China will be the first country in the world to do so. By mid-2020, China plans to launch a Mars mission, with three components: an orbiter, a lander, and a rover.[29] By 2022, China's most important space achievement will take place — its own space station will be operational.[30]

A space station is a dual accomplishment for China. Along with being the only country to have its own manned space station, China's space station will have its version of the Hubble telescope. China's version will be 300 times bigger, however, with the potential to map 40 percent of the known universe within ten years.[31] By 2036, China wants to conduct a manned Moon landing,[32] and between 2040 and 2060, a manned mission to Mars.[33]

China's space plans and ambitions are grandiose, and Beijing is rapidly turning those plans into reality. As China makes its dreams come true, to whom will they listen? To whom should they listen?

Take Mars as an example. Today, nobody controls the planet. The United States operates the only rover on Mars, which is being used to look for signs of life, such as water. In the future, countries may use rovers and orbiters to identify zones for future human missions. With China planning to launch its Mars mission by mid-2020, it's possible that in the 2020s, other countries, such as Canada, Germany, or

Japan, will send their own orbiters to Mars. Each country can use their orbiters to identify areas for humans to settle in the future. But, who can claim which territory? Suppose the Chinese and Japanese rovers and orbiters on Mars identify the same area for future human settlement. To which country does it belong?

Because the UN already has an Outer Space Treaty, it may be considered the only institution that has a model to guide space matters. But it's no secret that the UN is a Western institution. China may not abide by a UN ruling on Mars.

Due to paranoia, geopolitical rivalry, and a lack of policy, China could ignore Japan's claim. It could make preparations to build its human settlement and announce to the world the location of China's manned base on Mars. This risks stoking anxieties between China and Japan. It could cause tensions in space that reverberate down to Earth. If China ignores Japan on Mars, Japan may turn around and ignore China on Earth. Both countries claim disputed islands in the East China Sea, known as the Senkaku/Diaoyu Islands. Japan claims sovereignty over the islands, yet China continues to dispute it. If China ignores Japan on Mars, Japan could begin building structures and bases on the disputed islands.

All of a sudden, tensions in space could make their way to Earth, and do so in a way that could lead to dangerous consequences. With no forum to negotiate a settlement or find common ground, every country will be operating independently with its own strategy, regardless of whether it collides with or challenges the strategies of other countries.

Resource Rivalry

Countries will definitely face challenges in resolving territory disputes in space, but these problems will become even harder to resolve if resources are involved.

For years, China has been taking steps on Earth to secure its energy supply and needs. It's building huge amounts of infrastructure in Africa, such as roads, stadiums, and more in exchange for access to resources. In Asia, China is deploying a "String of Pearls" strategy, building its own ports and infrastructure in the Indian Ocean and Southeast Asia to secure resources from the Middle East.[34]

China is also looking at unconventional energy sources to add to its energy mix. One of them is nuclear fusion. Nuclear fusion energy requires one of two isotopes: deuterium (found in water) and tritium (not found in nature).[35] But there's a third isotope, called helium-3, that can enable nuclear fusion. The problem is that this isotope is rare on Earth.

It is not, however, rare on the Moon. The Moon is calculated to have 1.1 million metric tons of helium-3 on its surface and in the ground. China is already planning missions to bring back lunar samples to analyze for helium-3.[36]

In the future, China could establish a mining base on the Moon to secure and utilize helium-3. If China could develop the technology for this, however, it won't be alone —the United States, Russia, Japan, and others could follow suit. As several countries prepare mining operations on the Moon to extract helium-3, who decides which country extracts where — especially if one area of the Moon has more helium-3 than another? If Japan and China identify the same section of the Moon in which to begin their mining operations, how will it be decided which country can mine where?

Under this scenario, Japan and China could agree to use the same area and build their mining sites in proximity to each other. But after months of operating, China could accuse Japan of stealing helium-3 or claim that the area has become unstable due to Japanese mining activity.

The scenario between China and Japan is one type of resource rivalry — directly between countries. What happens when companies get involved?

In December 2015, the United States passed the Space Act of 2015. It reduced the red tape around private companies launching rockets. More importantly, it gave private companies the "… property rights to the resources they mine from asteroids … ."[37] In other words, the resources that SpaceX or Planetary Resources mine from an asteroid are theirs to keep — they belong to no other nation or economy. This is a big deal for companies. Consider that in July 2015, an asteroid containing 90 million tons of platinum and other materials passed by Earth. The price tag of these resources? Between $300 billion and $5.4 trillion.[38]

The 1967 Outer Space Treaty includes a rule stating that, "States shall be responsible for national space activities whether carried out by governmental or non-governmental entities." Basically, the U.S. government is liable for the actions of SpaceX, Planetary Resources, and other American companies, even though these companies are not part of the U.S. government.

Tomorrow, U.S.-based Planetary Resources could begin mining and transporting resources from an asteroid in proximity to Earth. At the same time, a Chinese space mining company could also begin mining that asteroid for resources. Here, the same set of challenges emerge. First, which company can claim the resources on the asteroid? Second, what happens if a set of tensions emerge?

If the miners that the Chinese company uses on the asteroid are damaged by the debris from the American miners, under the UN's Outer Space Treaty, the United States is liable. How would China react if such an incident were to occur? Turn the tables. How would the United States react if China's mining machines damage American mining machines? What makes these questions important isn't just the geopolitical complexity of it, but that such tensions are not a result of anything a government has a done. It's companies and their conduct that could lead to future geopolitical conflict.

Are countries ready for geopolitical tensions fueled by the actions of companies?

Space Power & Economy

While space presents its own geopolitical challenges, it's also a geopolitical opportunity. Two countries have taken note of this: China and Luxembourg.

In August 2016, China launched a quantum science satellite, known as Quantum Experiments at Space Scale (QUESS). This satellite is capable of bringing a new kind of security and cryptography to Earth through quantum entanglement.[39] Essentially, quantum entanglement is " ... the act of fusing two or more particles into quantum states ... ." When this state is observed, it collapses. In other words, if two people are having an email conversation and a third person or entity tries to read it, the email conversation disappears. QUESS could allow China to bring a new Chinese encryption to Earth.

How is this an opportunity for China? As mentioned previously, China is building huge amounts of infrastructure throughout Africa. As China builds, it is strengthening its relationship with African governments, giving China a huge hold on African affairs. Tomorrow, China could expand its infrastructure building in Africa to include Internet and security. China could also promise African nations and their populations a new kind of security through Chinese satellites.

In the future, China's quantum satellite experiments will likely go beyond encryption to include beaming down Internet from satellites. China can offer this to populations in Africa, along with Asia, the Middle East, and South America. This is China's way of challenging American Internet dominance in the world (underwater cables). Today, a majority of the world's Internet passes through the United States. Tomorrow, will it pass through China's satellites?

Another opportunity that space presents is in growing the economy of countries, such as Luxembourg — a small European country that has traditionally grown its economy through banking.

In February 2016, Luxembourg announced a strategy to take its economy in a new direction. Seeking to become a leader in space mining, the country is set to establish a financial and regulatory environment that attracts space mining companies.[40] In June 2016, Luxembourg unveiled plans to set up a $223 million fund for space mining initiatives.[41]

Luxembourg is embracing the future by setting itself up to become a global hub for space mining operations and launches. As it moves to have space mining fuel its economy, what will space mining mean for Luxembourg's place in the global economy?

Mineable resources on planets and asteroids will have price tags in the hundreds of billions, if not trillions, of dollars. If Luxembourg is one of the few countries with the capabilities to launch space mining operations, it could develop and launch its own state-backed companies into space to mine objects. Two challenges could arise, however.

The first challenge is economic. Luxembourg could mine trillions of dollars worth of oil, natural gas, metals, and more, and then bring them back to Earth and sell them on world markets. How would this be calculated? Would Luxembourg's GDP, which as of 2016 was only $60 billion, now surpass the trillion dollar mark because of the goods it mines in space?

The second challenge is geopolitical. If Luxembourg were to sell resources on world markets, that would mean it would be competing to sell resources. This could pit Luxembourg against established resource powers like Russia, Iran, Qatar, and Saudi Arabia. Is Luxembourg ready for this? Equally important, are energy powers expecting disruption in this form?

In addition, space mining would create a new economy. In the future, when SpaceX prepares to mine an asteroid, several things could take place. From the moment SpaceX begins mining the asteroid, people in stock markets would bet on how big a yield will be found — $50 billion, $200 billion, or $500 billion. After the mining operation is completed, SpaceX may open up its yield to buyers from around the world. All of a sudden, a new product worth hundreds of billions (or trillions) is being sold on the world markets.

Who will regulate these space economies? No single country can. The United States will want its own rules, as will Russia, China, and every other country. Just like when it came to territory, institutions will be ignored due to geopolitical alignment and paranoia.

Will countries cooperate to create a space-based organization that governs economic conduct? Or will countries operate using their own independent rules, clashing, and lobbying, with the rest of the world?

Conclusion

Alongside China, many countries are pursuing advances in space.

Currently, the United States continues as the dominant force in space. In a report, NASA proposes using remote-controlled robotic droids to construct a moon base by 2024.[42] At the same time, the Pentagon has contracted a space company to develop robotic arms for repairing satellites orbiting Earth.[43] In addition, the International Space Station (ISS) has begun the process of creating a solar-system wide Internet system.[44]

Indian space capabilities became famous in 2013, when India sent an orbiter to Mars for just $74 million, compared to the $671 million it cost the United States for the same undertaking.[45] Immediately after the successful launch of India's Mars orbiter, the Indian Space Research Organization (IRSO) proposed Venus as its next destination.[46] ISRO has set a goal of launching sixty space missions over the next five years, or twelve missions every year.[47] Already, ISRO has launched satellites for more than fifty countries, including Luxembourg, Turkey, Denmark, and France.[48]

South Korea has unveiled its space strategy, called Space Vision 2040.[49] Under this plan, the country aims to have an orbiter on the moon by 2020, and a native astronaut in space onboard a South Korean shuttle by 2040. Japan's Aerospace Exploration Agency (JAXA) has set an objective to have a manned lunar base by 2030.[50] Plans include sending humans in 2020 to build the base, which is expected to take until 2030 to complete. By the 2030s, JAXA envisions beaming solar power down to Earth through a Space Solar Power System (SSPS).[51] Also in the 2030s, Russia plans to have its own Moon base,[52] and Nigeria wants to send its own astronaut into space.[53]

When it comes to space, every country has its own specific objective — for some, it's economic diversification, while for others it's national security, soft power, or a mix of different things. For these countries, the strategy and execution may be clear — but are the consequences? Who will set the rules for space conduct? To whom will countries turn when they face an issue? Who has the right to call the shots?

Today, policy is lacking when it comes to space. No map, compass, or history exists on which to fall back.

Countries will clash over territory and resources. Businesses will cause headaches for their governments. The world will become more polarized. At the same time, space will be utilized to expand influence on Earth and grow the economy.

Countries must begin preparing now. Unlike on Earth, where the borders, cultures, and map are known, space is a no-man's-land. The final frontier is up for grabs.

Who will claim it?

Chapter 3

Dangerous Automation
Will automation break the world?

New York City, United States
January 2027

Leaders of the countries that are part of the reformed United Nations Security Council (UNSC) are debating over how to best solve the protests and revolts taking place over automation. The air in the room is stuffy. Words have been spoken, voices have been raised. The stakes are high.

Japan's president recently escaped an assassination attempt by an angry mob of workers who breached the motorcade in which he was traveling. The American president is worried over states, such as Texas and Colorado, holding independence referendums to create their own economic policies toward automation. Within two weeks, France will run out of money to fund its universal basic income scheme, which it has been using to help people affected by automation.

The remaining countries of the UNSC — India, Brazil, Germany, Britain, Canada, Russia, and China — are all facing their own social, political, and economic challenges dealing with automation and the job losses stemming from it.

Japan's president proposes that UNSC members create an economic fund to create basic income schemes. American, Brazilian, Indian, and Chinese leaders agree. The European leaders, Russia, and Canada reject this proposal. They don't have the financial means and liquidity to contribute any significant amount.

The debate continues for the next hour and a half. During that time, the UNSC is briefed on violent protests taking place in Beijing. Hundreds of thousands of workers who have lost their jobs to automation are calling for a new, democratic government to tackle the economic challenges facing the country.

After more than four hours of discussion, the leaders get up. They can't agree on a plan. Just as the leaders leave the room, the German Chancellor makes one final comment.

"How did automation become so dangerous, so fast — and none of us saw this coming?"

Introduction

According to experts, three waves of industrial automation have occurred.[54] The first wave began in the 1970s, when automation technology was used by the automotive sector to put together parts. The second wave started at the beginning of the 21st century, as service robots made their way into the world.[55] Experts claim the third wave is taking place now, and it revolves around human–robot coexistence in the workplace, a type of industrial automation. In 2014, industrial automation had already gained so much ground that if it were measured as its own country, it would be the 53rd largest economy in the world.[56]

As this third wave of automation rolls out, will it go as planned? Or instead of working with humans, will robots just replace us?

Take a look at Japan. It's the world's third largest economy, with a population of 126.2 million and a labor force of more than 65 million.[57] Late in 2015, researchers at the Japanese consulting firm, Nomura Research Institute (NRI), released a study that analyzed the effects of robots on the Japanese job market. They found that up to 49 percent of jobs in Japan could be replaced by machines.[58] If NRI's projections are correct, more than 30 million people in Japan could be out of work due to automation.

Move to the West — the Bank of England conducted a study focusing on the job market in the United States and United Kingdom, and projected that a total of 95 million jobs between the two countries were at risk of being replaced by robots.[59] That translates to a potential 50 percent of the workforce in the United States and United Kingdom being replaced by automation.[60]

Powerful institutions are also stepping in to sound a global alarm about automation. In 2016, the Switzerland-based World Economic Forum (WEF) projected that 5 million jobs in fifteen developed and developing countries were at risk of disappearing over the next five years because of the "fourth industrial revolution."[61]

These projections paint a grim picture. Are they far from the truth?

Some people believe the risk of automation is overblown. They point to the past as evidence. In the 19th century, 25 percent of all agricultural jobs were in threshing grain — separating grain from the plant. This job was automated in the 1860s.[62] When the first wave of automation struck the automotive industry in the 1970s, an estimated one in seven US jobs was connected to the auto industry.[63] Many of these jobs ended up being automated, but the U.S. economy didn't break down. As the argument goes, since the world survived these waves of automation, why couldn't it survive the coming waves?

Perhaps this argument is correct. But even if history is simply repeating itself and the world passes through this current wave of automation largely unscathed, it doesn't mean we shouldn't prepare for the worst and understand what could take place. Are governments ready to deal with automation on a global scale? What are their strategies? What does this all mean for the future of the world?

Universal Basic Income

Today, many governments are pursuing universal basic income (UBI) schemes.

In late 2015, officials from the Netherlands city of Utrecht announced plans for a basic income program in the future. Under it, people would be paid £660 per month.[64] In Finland, the government directed its social insurance agency Kela to " ... carry out experiments ... " on basic income to identify the advantages.[65] The Canadian province of Ontario included a pilot for a basic income scheme in its provincial budget in early 2016 to help people living below the poverty line.[66]

One of the most famous UBI schemes was proposed in Switzerland. In June 2016, Switzerland held a long-awaited referendum on introducing a monthly basic income scheme. It was defeated — 77 percent of voters rejected it. If the referendum had passed, it would have resulted in every adult in Switzerland receiving $2,555 per month, and every child receiving close to $645 per month. The money would arrive regardless of whether an adult was working.[67]

Today, governments and people are pursuing UBI to advance their societies and economies. Tomorrow, these same schemes could be deployed to help deal with automation — but they may not be sustainable.

In January 2016, Citigroup and the Oxford Martin School published a report using data from the World Bank. They found that countries that were part of the Organization for Economic Co-operation and Development (OECD) faced, on average, the risk of 57 percent of all jobs being automated.[68]

For other countries, the job-automation risk was higher. Ethiopia for example, showed an 85 percent risk; China, 77 percent; and Thailand, 72 percent. Other countries included India, with a 69 percent risk; South Africa, with 67 percent; Nigeria and Argentina, each with 65 percent; and the United States, with 47 percent.

The United States has a labor force of about 161 million people. If the projections from Citigroup and Oxford are accurate more than 75 million American jobs are at risk. Should this prediction come true, it'll result in tens of millions of Americans being out of work in the coming years. To deal with this tsunami of unemployment, the U.S. government may create a basic income scheme. For example, people who lose their job to automation (hardware and/or software) may receive $1500 per month.

As in other countries, the problem is that a basic income scheme in the United States would be funded by the government. For governments, the main source of revenue is personal income tax (termed individual income tax in the United States). For the United States alone, personal income tax represents 47% of the government's revenue.[69] Another tax for U.S. citizens is payroll tax, which is deducted from the salary earned by most people in the country, and accounts for another 33 percent of U.S. government revenue. This means an estimated 80 percent of all government revenue in the United States comes from working people. It is important to note that people only pay these their personal and payroll tax if they're employed.

This creates an enormous obstacle for the future of UBI schemes around the world. As more and more people lose work to automation, governments make less money. How will they keep basic income programs alive?

One strategy is to take on debt. But this means many countries would increase their debt loads to unsustainable levels. As of 2015, world debt stood at $60 trillion,[70] while the world GDP was over $113 trillion.[71] Is permanent, out-of-proportion debt — fueled by automation — the future of the global economy?

Another strategy is to sell debt. In April 2016, Belgium followed Ireland in issuing a 100-year bond to help deal with economic challenges.[72] But, a 100-year bond is essentially an investment in a completely unknown future. In the past, five- or ten-year bonds were considered risky. One hundred years from now, a country like Belgium or Ireland may no longer exist in its current form or shape — or at all.[73] Is selling debt with these timelines just another way to avoid dealing with the problem today?

If UBI schemes struggle to take off, governments will have to look at alternative methods to deal with the dangerous effects of automation. What else can they do?

Productivity Tax

An alternative to a UBI is to begin taxing the automation technologies themselves. One concept is that of a "productivity tax" — a tax on machines and software based on a business's productivity.[74]

If implemented, what could this look like?

In May 2016, Adidas announced it would relaunch shoe manufacturing in Germany by 2017.[75] Most of the employees will be machines, however, not people. At the same time, a report published in 2015 projected that 59 percent of the German workforce could be replaced by machines and software in the future.[76]

The German government needs a solution to regulate automation and raise revenue in new ways. One option would be to introduce a productivity tax of 30 percent, which would charge Adidas and other companies based on the productivity boost machines provide to the company.

But how is productivity calculated? One way to calculate it is to base it on how much money a company saves when it employs machines over workers. For example, if the Adidas shoe factory were to save $5 million each day by employing robots instead of humans, the productivity tax of 30 percent would bring $1.5 million per day to the government.

Alternatively, the productivity tax could be calculated based on the projected value of the goods the machines manufacture above what was being manufactured by humans. Under this strategy, if the shoe factory were to produce 40 percent more goods per day due to robots, it may have a projected value of $3 million. In this case, the German government would receive

$900,000 daily when applying the 30 percent productivity tax.

Either way, Adidas could face a new tax in Germany for using automation technologies instead of people. The new challenges don't end here, however. While the German government would have solved automation from a public policy front, it would now face another problem: How would it keep Adidas from leaving the country and moving to a country with no productivity tax?[77]

Adidas could pick up and move to Brazil — which may not have a productivity tax — and there would be little the German government could do to stop it. If Brazil were to actively lobby companies to relocate there and operate productivity-tax free, Germany may be forced to treat this as a geopolitical matter.

Germany could respond by putting restrictions on goods manufactured outside the country by machines instead of by German labor, or it could limit imports from countries that are perceived to be taking businesses out of Germany — in this case, Brazil.

Alternatively, governments could pursue limiting automation altogether, or introducing "automation quotas." Under this concept, a country like South Africa could introduce a quota requiring companies to only use automation for 25 percent of their labor requirements. Humans would have to be employed for the remaining 75 percent. This would give rise to the same challenge, however: How would South Africa keep companies from leaving and moving to countries without automation quotas?

In short, countries can't stop companies from leaving. If they try, either by taking on the companies or taking on the countries to which the companies have moved, it could start new geopolitical tensions. Will automation create the next diplomatic problems or court cases between corporations and governments?

Coming Revolutions

As governments struggle to find the right solution for automation, people will be caught in the crossfire. This could lead to chaos in societies around the world. China is one society that faces a high risk from automation.

In late 2015, Chinese Vice President Li Yuanchao unveiled a plan to replace millions of workers in China with machines.[78] At the same time, China's Guangdong Province, which is short 600,000 to 800,000 workers, has earmarked US$154 billion in funding to fuel automation. The provincial capital, Guangzhou, has set its own goal. By 2020, it aims to automate 80 percent of the city's manufacturing.[79]

The president of the China Machinery Industry Federation said in July 2016 that China plans to be part of the top-ten ranking by 2020 when it comes to automation. The plan is to do this by fueling domestic robot production and increasing robot density, which is calculated based on the number of robots per 10,000 workers. Currently, robot density in China is 36 to 10,000. By 2020, the goal is to increase this to 150 to 10,000.[80]

This entire automation strategy is taking place alongside plans to lay off 5 million to 6 million state workers in China over the next two to three years. To cope with this, the government has put aside $23 billion for support programs.[81] In other words, China is both fueling automation and laying off workers. The government expects to retrain these workers and employ them in different sectors.

Does China have a magic formula to pull this off? The Chinese economy isn't doing as well as it once was. It only grew 6.9 percent in 2015 — the slowest growth rate in twenty-five years.[82] One of the biggest risks to China's dual strategy is that the millions of people who lose their jobs may not want to go back to work in a factory — or they won't be able to find work at all. What will the people who cannot find work — or who want to find different work but can't — do, especially if they measure in the hundreds of thousands (or millions)?

The Chinese government appears to be aware of this risk. In June 2016, researchers in

Canada published their findings about censorship in China. One area being censored on WeChat, a popular messaging platform with hundreds of millions of users in China, involved messages having to do with robots taking human jobs.[83] Is the Chinese government using digital platforms to limit paranoia about the risk that automation presents to the Chinese job market?

Without a sound plan, China could be stepping into dangerous territory when it comes to automation. Leaving millions of people at risk of being unemployed could force them to revolt against the government, either in Beijing or in the provincial capitals. Is automation laying the seeds for the next Chinese revolution?

New Jobs

While automation presents multiple risks and challenges for governments and populations around the world, it also has an often-overlooked advantage: People will have more free time and more capabilities at their fingertips.

A lawn-mowing company could employ multiple robotic lawn mowers instead of manually operating the mowers. This would allow the company to complete more lawn jobs in the same time span, allowing for more business.[84]

A father or mother raising a young child at home could use a robot to entertain or teach the child while the parent works. Perhaps they would use robotic technologies at work too, like 3D printing goods or maintaining a chatbot to answer complex questions regarding the stock market.

In the same report in which the WEF projected that automation will lead to 5 million jobs disappearing by 2020, another projection stated that 2 million new jobs will be created in the same time span.[85] Will automation play a part in this?

The report from the NRI, mentioned earlier in the chapter, also stated that jobs having to do with creativity and compassion will be hard to automate. This could be an indicator of the kinds of jobs and industries that will remain human-centric — like sales, customer service, and other related fields.

If automation creates new jobs and industries, this may be the answer to why it has not created chaos throughout the world in the past. Perhaps automation has forced humans to invent and innovate in profound ways. What, then, is on the horizon for jobs and industry in the current and future waves of automation?

Conclusion

Will automation break the world? This is the question in front of governments, companies, and people all over the planet.

Different strategies are being explored. Some appear more extreme than others. In May 2016, a motion entered the European Union to label robotic workers as "electronic persons," and make the owners or employers of these robots culpable for social security payments. The goal is to give advanced robots their own "rights and obligations."[86] Is the European Union laying down a public policy blueprint for the rest of the world to adopt?

Alongside government strategy is the immediate challenge of what people will do after they're replaced by automation if no safety net or structure is in place to help them. Will they become dependent on the welfare system, or will they grow angry and revolt against a government they feel has been incompetent in planning for the future?

As all this volatility takes hold, automation may lead to the creation of the next industries and jobs, creating brand new opportunities for people, countries, and businesses.

In other words, there's no one-size-fits-all solution for automation. The effects of automation will be completely dependent on the country.

For a country like Ethiopia, where Citigroup and Oxford projected that 85 percent of jobs are at risk from automation, the government may not have the means of introducing a basic income scheme. It won't want to tax companies for fear of losing them. Will Ethiopia break down because of automation?

Meanwhile, developed countries will face an equally daunting challenge. People have gotten used to a certain quality of life in these countries, and economies have run based on expectations of how much people and companies will earn and spend. Are developed countries in for a rude awakening?

No one knows, and that's why it is important to pay attention to automation and the projections around it. No one can project how large or how small the effects of automation will be on the world.

Perhaps the experts were wrong about the waves of automation. Instead of being in a third wave, we're actually at the beginning of a fourth wave, where automation will challenge every preconceived notion of work, life, and government.

Chapter 4

Food Cloning
Is free trade coming to an end?

Geneva, Switzerland
July 2041

The WTO director-general is sitting in her office, reviewing proposals from senior staff on how best to solve an ongoing trade dispute between France and Italy over red wine. Suddenly, her phone rings. It's her secretary, who informs the director-general that she has received an anonymous tip on Brazil's future trade strategy.

By 2043, Brazil plans to become the world's leading tea exporter. The plan is to accomplish this by using food-cloning technology. This technology allows Brazil to clone tea crops domestically in massive quantities, and export them to other countries. These crops can be customized for flavor, fusions, and more.

The director-general's mind begins to race. This isn't the first time the WTO has dealt with food cloning. In 2035, Spain challenged the United States by cloning oranges and flooding the U.S. market with Spanish oranges. Without intervention from the WTO, the United States moved forward with a 40 percent tax on all Spanish imports, due to the effect Spanish oranges were having on states like Florida.

How will Brazil's tea strategy affect countries that depend on tea exports?

Again, the phone rings. The director-general's secretary tells her that Sri Lanka has caught wind of Brazil's plans. The Sri Lankan minister of industry and commerce is on the line, and is worried.

Tea is Sri Lanka's biggest export.

Introduction

The world today is more interconnected and interdependent than at any point in human history. At the end of 2015, 3.2 billion people were on the Internet, accounting for 43.4 percent of the world's population.[87] The UN wants to increase this percentage to 60 percent by 2020. As more people become connected, the global economy continues to grow. In 2006, the World Bank projected that the global economy would reach $72 trillion by 2030. In 2014, sixteen years earlier, the global economy was valued at $77 trillion.[88]

One of the biggest drivers of this growing interconnection and interdependence is free trade, whereby any restrictions to trade, such as tariffs and duties, are removed. With fewer restrictions for trade, the ability for countries to sell to the world grows.

Most of the time, trade deals and agreements have geopolitical motives behind them. An example of this is the Regional Comprehensive Economic Partnership (RCEP). This is a proposed free-trade agreement between ASEAN — comprised of ten countries in Southeast Asia — and India, China, Japan, South Korea, New Zealand, and Australia.

If RCEP is implemented, it will include more than 3 billion people (45 percent of the world's population) and will have a combined GDP of $23 trillion (a third of the world's economy).[89] The agreement would balance the global playing field, giving Asian countries the ability to compete with the West. It's also viewed as a rival to the Trans-Pacific Partnership (TPP), an American-led trade deal that includes countries in Asia-Pacific region.

Free trade can be disrupted in several ways. If a country wants to protect a local industry, it can limit imports from another country, like what happened during the U.S.–Canada softwood lumber dispute. Free trade can also be disrupted when a country wants to expand its economic power by manipulating its exports. This is what China is being accused of when it artificially lowers the Yuan to make its exports cheaper.

Now, another trade disruption is on the horizon. It revolves around the ability of countries to clone food like plants and animals — products they once imported. What will food cloning mean for world trade? How will countries protect their exports? How will food cloning affect the way the world operates?

Cows & Coffee

Cloning raises a lot of eyebrows — and fears — because it is usually affiliated with human cloning, whereby one person can produce multiple versions of himself or herself for various reasons.[90] Cloning has applications beyond humans, however. One of them is the ability to clone animals and plants, such as cows and coffee.

For many countries, exporting animals and plants is a huge part of their economies. If these exports decline, their economies are at risk of collapsing. Argentina's biggest export is soybeans. For Sri Lanka, it's tea. Uruguay depends on beef, while Senegal relies on fish.[91]

Until now, countries have struggled with exports because they don't have the infrastructure to export certain goods, the market is oversupplied, or geopolitics limits what they can sell. What happens when countries have to compete with other countries cloning goods locally instead of importing them?

One export that is at risk from food cloning is beef. As of 2016, the world's five largest beef exporters were, in descending order: India, Brazil, Australia, the United States, and New Zealand.[92] For India, where cows are considered holy and not to be killed, beef exports have overtaken basmati rice as the country's largest agriculture export.[93] Yesterday, India knew its competition and had a strategy to compete. Tomorrow, India's beef competition can come in a way that was never expected.

In 2015, BoyaLife Genomics, a biotechnology company from China, announced plans to construct a factory in Tianjin. It'll be the size of three football fields. Inside, BoyaLife plans to clone 100,000 cows per year, eventually reaching 1 million per year by 2020.[94] The initial cloning goal of 100,000 cows annually is six times the size of the largest cattle ranches in the United States.[95]

BoyaLife is so confident in its cloning capabilities that the company's CEO said it already has the technology to clone humans.[96] Currently, BoyaLife is investing in cow cloning to supply the growing demand for beef in China. In the coming decades, BoyaLife and other such companies in China may decide to supply a global beef demand, as well.

How does India respond to this? China cloning cows domestically and exporting them abroad will cut into Indian beef exports.

Another export at risk from food cloning is coffee. Every year, more than 400 billion cups of coffee are consumed around the world. In the United States alone, an estimated 100 million people drink 350 million cups of coffee every day.[97]

Brazil is the largest coffee-producing country in the world. Its coffee industry employs more than five million people and provides 40 percent of the world's coffee supply. Vietnam is the second largest producer of coffee, providing 16 percent of the total world supply and employing one million people. An estimated 25 percent of Columbia's rural population is employed by the coffee sector, while in Indonesia, the coffee sector is supplied by 1.5 million people working on small farms.[98] Coffee is the biggest export for Guatemala, El Salvador, Nicaragua, Ethiopia, Uganda, Rwanda, Burundi, and Madagascar.[99]

In 2008, Nestle created clones of the Robusta coffee plant, another blend of coffee like Arabica. The company planned to distribute these clones to coffee growers globally.[100]

In 2011, the Department of Agriculture in the Philippines began testing Nestle coffee-plant clones to stimulate domestic coffee production. Three areas were selected to test the clones. One of them was Bukidnon, a landlocked province located in Southern Philippines.

The Philippines imports 50,000 metric tons of coffee beans every year. If Nestle coffee plants work, Bukidnon alone would provide a larger yield than what the Philippines imports.[101] As of 2014, the Philippines imported 70 percent of its coffee beans from three countries: Indonesia, Thailand, and Vietnam.[102]

The Philippines is laying the foundation for future coffee independence. But as they do this, they're putting their trade partners in a tough situation. How do Indonesia, Thailand, and Vietnam — along with the other countries that export coffee to the Philippines — compete with the Philippines cloning coffee plants instead of importing coffee?

The Geopolitics of Food Cloning

As more countries adopt food cloning, it will begin to have geopolitical implications.

As India and China compete over beef exports, China could use its beef exports to hurt

India economically. The Chinese government could subsidize the entire program, with no regard for profit, to use cheap beef exports to flood global markets and make it harder and harder for India to sell its beef. China could also license its cow-cloning technology to countries that import Indian beef. These countries could pay China an annual royalty, or give resources to China in exchange for the ability to clone cows domestically instead of buying them from abroad. Is India prepared for either scenario?

Countries could also use cloning to attack the economy of other countries.

For example, if Spain and the United States are embroiled in a serious dispute that threatens relations, Spain could deploy food cloning to get back at the United States. In this scenario, Spain could clone oranges in massive quantities and flood the American market with cheap Spanish oranges. The goal would be to hurt U.S. states like Florida, where oranges are an important part of the economy.

Food cloning will also fuel new organizations, while challenging existing ones. Countries affected by food cloning could band together and create a new governing institution for trade, such as United Against Food Cloning. This group could set standardized trade rules, such as prohibiting using cloning technologies for trade purposes. It could also create a set of exports that can be cloned, while everything else would have to be traded using traditional methods.

At the same time, organizations like the WTO will face challenges. In late 2015, the WTO discussed a proposed EU-ban on " ... products derived from cloned animals ... " The United States and Brazil called such a ban trade-restrictive.[103]

Using the example in which Indonesia, Vietnam, and Thailand lose out to Filipino-cloned coffee plants, these three countries could file a complaint with the WTO. Indonesia, Vietnam, and Thailand could claim that the Philippines' cloning technology interferes with their coffee exports reaching the Filipino market. How would the WTO respond to a complaint like this — especially if countries around the world begin filing similar complaints?

Alternatively, Indonesia, Thailand, or Vietnam could restrict Filipino exports in their countries by adding tariffs and duties. This could lead to a trade dispute in Southeast Asia between several countries. This trade dispute could become even more complicated, because all four countries are part of ASEAN. Could food cloning fracture political organizations?

Equally important is what the populations negatively affected by food cloning would do. People employed by sectors that export goods now being cloned in other countries are at a high risk of losing their jobs. If many countries around the world follow the Philippines' example and begin cloning coffee plants locally, it could take an increasing bite out of the coffee exports of traditional distributors like Brazil and Vietnam.

Again, the coffee sector employs five million people in Brazil and one million people in Vietnam. If the plants and farms that employ these people see sales drop because countries no longer import as much, these plants and farms will be forced to lay off workers. Even if only 30 percent of the coffee workers in both countries lose work due to food cloning, that's 1.5 million people in Brazil and 300,000 people in Vietnam out of work. Will these people sit idle, or will they grow angry at their governments for not taking steps to protect their jobs?

The impact on farmers and agriculture is the biggest consequence of cloning.

It may take years for cloned goods to affect world trade. However, when countries stop or reduce exports, it's immediately felt by both workers and businesses.

For governments and populations, the biggest challenge in responding to food cloning is that, unlike in the past — when a change in economic policy or an innovative government could create jobs — when it comes to food cloning, no change of government or revolution will bring back jobs replaced by cloning. A country that loses jobs to food cloning cannot tell another country to stop cloning goods and start importing them.

Those jobs are gone forever.

Conclusion

For decades, governments have pursued trade with the end goal of having their goods accessed by the world. Most trade-related fears revolved around a country limiting exports or a regime breaking down. Little thought has been given to what else could disrupt trade, such as food cloning.

One of the fundamental challenges that food cloning brings to the world stage is that, traditionally, trade has long been external — taking place in the air or on the ocean's surface. This allowed institutions like the WTO and others to dictate the rules. Trade activity happened in international areas that everyone used, accessed, and needed.

But cloning is internal — it takes place inside countries. Who can tell a country what they can and cannot do, even if what they're doing is affecting the global system as a whole?

As institutions struggle to find their feet in a trade system being disrupted by food cloning, countries will grapple with how to respond when cloning threatens their economy.

There's also the question of why certain countries will adopt cloning. For developed nations, cloning provides a new industry to grow the economy. For developing nations, cloning allows them to reduce their dependence on other countries.

As years go by, the technologies and capabilities around cloning will only advance. This means that countries have a finite amount of time to develop plans and strategies for food cloning.

Trade used to allow countries to grow their economy, integrate with the global economy, and stimulate their geopolitical power. In the future, trade may hinder countries, fracture the global economy, and shift geopolitical power.

Chapter 5

New Rules of War
Redefining Responsibility

Canberra, Australia
August 1, 2030

The Australian prime minister is woken up. The security team rushes the PM to a briefing room, where cabinet ministers and military staff are already seated. The minister of foreign affairs stands up to speak.

"At 3 a.m. our time, our satellites picked up artillery fire between Chinese and Japanese navy vessels near the disputed Senkaku/Diaoyu Islands in the East China Sea. This incident is now escalating. China and Japan are moving more military assets into the region. Russian and Iranian forces are moving air assets to bases on China's eastern coast. Japan has issued an emergency request to the United States and NATO for immediate military support."

The minister pauses, glances at the prime minister, and then continues.

"Initial assessments from the Australian Secret Intelligence Service and our counterparts in the US, UK, and Israel propose that this incident was started by the malfunctioning of a Japanese autonomous missile system installed near the islands, designed to fire on a ship without human command. When a Chinese navy vessel moved into a certain radius, the missile system decided this radius was too close and launched missiles at the ship, destroying it and killing all crew members on board."

Once again, the minister pauses. She analyzes the prime minister's body language and facial expressions, and nervously asks, "Mr. Prime Minister, what should we do?"

Introduction

One area of a country where doctrine has not changed significantly over the past several decades is the military. For decades, militaries have evolved in their structure, capabilities and role, but their basic playbook has remained the same. If another country attacks its country, or if an ally is attacked, the military goes to war.

One reason why this operating doctrine hasn't evolved is because, until recently, the ways in which a country can launch an attack haven't changed significantly. Instead, the means of attack just got stronger.

Drones are replacing manned fighter jets, while delivering the same payload — missiles. Nuclear weapons remain the most destructive weapon, but they're now measured in relation to the atomic bombs dropped in Japan.

This doctrine is currently being disrupted. As countries leverage new technologies to improve their defensive and offensive capabilities, a new question must be asked: What constitutes an act of war?

In the past, this question was answered. If North Korea launched a cruise missile at Seoul or crossed the demilitarized zone with tens of thousands of troops, it would be considered an act of war by South Korea.

But what if both North Korea and South Korea were to simultaneously launch armed drones to monitor each other's borders — drones programmed to attack without human command — and these drones begin attacking each other? Does this constitute an act of war? Should it?

As new technologies make their way onto the battlefield, countries are going to face a tremendous amount of confusion. What risks do governments face in this new kind of battlefield, where there are no established rules or models to follow?

Autonomous Robots

Until recently, military robots have been controlled by humans. We input commands, push buttons, and program parameters. When the United States deployed the first robots in ground combat in Qiqay, Afghanistan, in 2002, they were remote-controlled by humans and sent into tunnels and caves to search for bombs and arms.[104]

Now, technology has reached a point where it can give military robots the ability to act independently and make decisions without human input. As of 2016, three countries are leading in this: the United States, Russia, and China.

In the United States, the Department of Defense is planning to create an autonomous weapons system controlled by an artificial intelligence that is able to decide when to attack someone, using predictive social media analytics.[105] The Pentagon, through its research and development wing, Defense Advanced Research Projects Agency (DARPA), has several projects underway to develop what is termed a lethal autonomous weapons system. One of these projects, Collaborative Operations in Denied Environment (CODE), seeks to develop aerial vehicles that can execute an entire mission on their own — target identification, tracking, attacking, and more.[106]

In June 2016, DARPA and the U.S. Navy sent a concept autonomous submarine into the ocean for testing. Dubbed Sea Hunter, it was developed to operate autonomously, with only specific tasks carried out by humans. It can even identify enemy submarines on its own.[107] A couple of months earlier in April, DARPA, along with several organizations, said it was working on creating autonomous self-driving vehicles for the military that could adapt to changing environmental conditions, such as incoming rocket fire.[108]

In 2014, Russia unveiled a robot tank called Wolf-2. It uses a technology called mobile robotic complex. When in automated mode, it can select targets on its own; however, at the time, firing was still controlled by humans.[109] In late 2015, a Russian state-owned company called United Instrument Manufacturing Corporation announced a software platform called Unicum, which gives robots, including military ones, artificial intelligence that allows them to make decisions on their own.[110] In one test, ten robots used Unicum and selected their leader.

China is working on developing advanced autonomous military robots for underwater applications in the South China Sea. Some call this strategy their Underwater Great Wall.[111] In June 2016, China shared some of its unmanned underwater vehicles at an exhibit. The exhibit revolved around using advanced sensors and autonomous vehicles underwater to track enemy ships and communicate with Chinese vessels. In April, China unveiled a separate, autonomous policing robot called AnBot, which can " … patrol autonomously and protect against violence or unrest … ."[112] It can help someone calling out for help, charge itself without human assistance, and — if needed — fire electroshock weapons and run over people.

As these autonomous technologies and others make their way into the world — and develop even more advanced capabilities — they'll shake up governments and force them to question whether they're responsible for the actions of these machines.

Autonomous Robot Policy

The US Deputy Secretary of Defense Robert Work addressed a national security forum in late 2015. Speaking on the state of China–Russia cooperation, he made a startling comment. He said the Pentagon was struggling to keep up with Chinese and Russian advancements around killer robots — military robots able to make decisions without human input.[113]

His comments came at a time when autonomous robots created fears for governments. One of the biggest fears is focused on who is responsible for the decisions these robots make on the battlefield.

In March 2016, officials from the U.S. Department of Defense publicly discussed the possibility of U.S. soldiers fighting alongside robots. They wanted to ensure the robots could operate autonomously without direct communication or command.[114]

In July, the U.S. military began using robot carts to patrol areas and watch for threats in Djibouti, the home of the U.S. military's African Command. Called Mobile Detection Assessment and Response Systems (MDARS), the robot carts can drive autonomously, scan areas using lasers, and more.115

Using MDARS instead of human soldiers helps the U.S. protect soldiers' lives. Djibouti has a border with Somalia, home of the terrorist group Al-Shabaab, and is across from Yemen, home of the terrorist group Al Qaeda, by water. In the future, the U.S. military may equip MDARS with the capability to make decisions on when to engage targets. If several MDARS observe children playing on the beach with cardboard guns, and identify them as threats and attack them, will the Djibouti government see this as an accident, or an attack? Either way, what action will the government take?

In 2014, Norway-based Kongsberg Defence & Aerospace developed a missile system that, when attached to a fighter jet, could control the weapons system and fire missiles without human interference.[116] Norway intercepted seventy-four Russian warplanes in

2014. The next time Norway scrambles its fighter jets equipped with the autonomous missile system, what are the risks?

Out of error, lack of data, or imprecise programming, the autonomous system could identify the Russian warplanes as invaders and immediate threats. Consequently, it could launch missiles to take them down. Within seconds, Norway would go from escorting Russian warplanes to firing at them, all because of an autonomous weapons system. When Russian officials find out what happened, will they consider it an accident or an act of war?

Autonomous military robots that can attack targets on their own are not decades away — they've already arrived. To deal with the threat this technology presents, governments are trying to create policy around it.

In April 2016, a UN meeting focused on regulation for autonomous military robots. Human Rights Watch, an international nongovernmental organization, called for guarantees that these robots would always be under the control of humans. For the most part, the discussion saw division between countries on how to deal with this technology. Pakistan called for a complete ban on such robots. The United Kingdom wanted to use current laws, and France proposed allowing autonomous robots to be able to identify their own targets.[117]

In the same month, during a Group of Seven (G7 — the world's seven most powerful industrialized countries: the United States, Japan, Germany, the United Kingdom, France, Italy, and Canada) meeting on technology, the Japanese communications minister called for developing eight basic rules to guide artificial intelligence development. The main focus of the rules was human control over artificial intelligence and " ... respect for human dignity and privacy ... ."[118] Is the G7 worried over the decisions artificial intelligence could make regarding the human race?

Difficulties will arise concerning autonomous military robots when it comes to an international policy framework, because this technology differs from advanced military technologies of the past. Unlike the nuclear weapons the world has actively been trying to control and limit, no country or body has been actively trying to limit advancements around autonomous military robots. This means that countries all over the world are developing them, using their own expertise, resources, and approval.

Because of this, autonomous military robots aren't just a concept — they already have a place within the military of several countries. A policy framework that bans such technology will not stop countries like the United States, Russia, and China from developing and deploying autonomous military robots, because they have already done so.

Equally important is how such a ban or limitation could be enforced. No country wants to have inferior military capabilities, and if autonomous military robots are the future, who'll give them up — especially if no one else does?

Without policy and understanding, autonomous military robots will create enormous challenges for countries around the world. As they're deployed and begin making decisions, diplomacy will become harder and harder to justify. Whether it's a Venezuelan autonomous military drone attacking citizens in Colombia during a surveillance mission, or a Polish autonomous tank using foreign software firing on its own troops, governments will be forced to enact measures that make it clear how to proceed once autonomous military robots make decisions, such as engaging a threat.

Underlying all this remains the most important question: Do the actions of autonomous military robots constitute an act of war?

Cyber Warfare

By now, the term cyber war or cyber attack is not unfamiliar. The sheer number and type of cyber attacks taking place across the world make it clear that a new age of warfare has begun.

For example, the US Office of Personnel Management (OPM) was hacked in 2015. Data on 21.5 million current and former federal employees was breached, including confidential health information on topics such as mental disorders and addictions.[119]

The main suspect in the hack? China. In December 2015, the Chinese government arrested individuals it claimed were affiliated with the OPM hack.[120] Chinese officials said the hack was carried out by criminals, not the state government.[121] Information later surfaced, revealing that Russia and China were working together to analyze the data from the breach to identify US spies and other people affiliated with covert operations.[122]

Now, cyber warfare is accelerating in new ways, once again raising the question of what constitutes an act of war.

In mid-2016, Iran was reported to be investigating a "...series of fires and oil explosions ..." that took place within its energy infrastructure. This, however, was not just an investigation into worker safety. Instead, Iran's Supreme Council of Cyberspace was involved, looking into whether these accidents were actually the result of a cyber attack.[123]

While Iran isn't new to being a target of advanced cyber attacks, such attacks that result in the deaths of workers are a new phenomenon. If the population of a country is now at risk from future cyber attacks, it will force governments to rethink how they respond.

In March 2016, the US government revealed that Iran had hacked into the Bowman Avenue Dam in New York.[124] While little damage was reported because the dam was offline, the hack reflects the vulnerability of critical infrastructure. If more accidents take place in Iran resulting in the deaths of workers, Tehran may decide to target the United States.

If Iran can hack into dams, can it also hack into water sanitation plants or power grids, either contaminating the water, shutting down the facilities, or overloading power circuits — creating an epidemic of sorts? If the United States uncovers that Iran was, in fact, behind this attack, will it justify a military campaign? Should it?

Strategy and response become even more blurry when one considers that future cyber attacks may not even be perpetrated by humans. In other words, what happens when the human element is taken out of cyber attacks?

In 2016, the annual Black Hat USA cybersecurity conference took place in Las Vegas. Within this conference was the DARPA Cyber Grand Challenge. The winner of the challenge developed autonomous systems to protect against cyber attacks. The objective of these systems was to scan a network or infrastructure, identify vulnerabilities, and fix them in real time.[125]

With this advancement came a risk, however. An expert mentioned that these same systems could be used to identify vulnerabilities and take advantage of them for nefarious purposes. Instead of protecting against cyber attacks, these autonomous systems could become the cyber attackers. This changes the entire equation when it comes to cyber warfare.

Autonomous entities, deployed by the government or nonstate actors to identify vulnerabilities within set parameters and breach them, change the future of cyber warfare. No longer are governments in control, the software is calling the shots. The decisions this software makes — like identifying a vulnerability in the traffic-light control system of a city and breaking into it to manipulate signals, causing widespread accidents, for example — will force governments to question their own responsibility.

Is South Africa responsible for an autonomous cyber-attacking entity that identifies a vulnerability in Nigeria's electrical grid, turning off power for millions, and like Stuxnet[126], physically damaging the infrastructure? Should Kazakhstan be held responsible for its autonomous cyber-attacking entity that identifies a vulnerability in the port control systems of Azerbaijan, creating logistical and economic chaos?

Countries may not be prepared for this kind of cyber warfare, in which attacks are no longer planned and executed by human beings. Instead, advanced artificial intelligence–based entities could be scouring the world, creating chaos and damaging infrastructure, all in the name of geopolitical supremacy.

Cyber Policy

Answers to the questions around who is responsible and what constitutes an act of war remain grey areas. For governments, no rules have been established, and that can mean the policies they enact are dangerous.

The North Atlantic Treaty Organization (NATO) is one of the world's most important defense blocs. Made up of twenty-eight member states, all based in Europe with the exception of the United States and Canada, NATO was formed in the 20th century to take on the Soviet Union. The most powerful doctrine NATO has is Article 5, which states that if any one member state is attacked, all member states go to war.

In the post-Soviet world, NATO has been struggling to align its defense strategy with new threats like cyber warfare. This struggle was initiated and exacerbated by several cyber attacks across Europe, with Russia being the suspect. One of the biggest attacks was on Ukraine's power grid, with 225,000 people losing power in December 2015. Reports later emerged, stating that hackers had access to the power-grid systems six months before they turned off the power.[127]

Another attack involved hackers breaking into computer systems in the German Parliament in 2015. The goal of the attack was to install software on the computers that would give the hackers permanent access to the systems, according to experts. In 2016, Germany's domestic intelligence agency blamed Russia for the attack.[128]

To thwart future cyber attacks, NATO announced in 2016 that it was considering changing the Article 5 policy to include cyber attacks. If approved, this will give NATO the power to declare war on a country that has executed a cyber attack against a NATO member.[129] What are the repercussions of this, especially if nonstate actors are taken into account?

If Germany and Russia were to deploy autonomous cyber-warfare entities to attack each other, and Russia's entity managed to break into the German stock exchange and cripple the market by taking it offline or manipulating prices, would NATO — of which Germany is a member — consider this an act of war? Should it?

Conclusion

Interfax reported in late 2014 that Russia was planning to deploy underwater-combat robots to protect oil rigs and transportation networks in the Arctic.[130] As the Arctic becomes a contested geopolitical battleground, many countries will likely deploy military vessels in the water. If Russia's underwater-combat robots were to identify one of the vessels as a threat — such as one from the United States — and fire on it, would this be considered an act of war?

India has put a Comprehensive Integrated Border Management System (CIBMS) into service in Punjab and Kashmir. It leverages several different technologies to guard the border at different points. The CIBMS combines thermal imaging, closed-circuit television cameras, battlefield surveillance radar, underground sensors, and laser walls.[131] If Pakistan were to launch a cyber attack on the CIBMS to disable it and allow insurgents to pass through India's border, would India consider this an act of war?

These questions are open-ended. There is no perfect answer. Depending on the conflict, country, ideology, and year, the response will be calculated differently.

For some people, the answer to whether these events constitute an act of war is "definitely." In their minds, an attack is an attack. It doesn't matter whether it comes from a human, a machine, or software.

For others, the answer is "definitely not." They believe an attack by a human is different from an attack by a machine or software. A human knows what she or he is doing, as well as the repercussions of those actions. A machine or software may have malfunctioned or been tampered with, however, making its decisions unpredictable.

Yet another group of people would respond, "it depends." They argue that at this time, countries should not be held responsible for the actions of technology, because the technology itself is still in its infancy. They feel countries should be held responsible by 2040 or 2050, because by then, the technology will be advanced enough to understand its consequences and risks.

Which group do you fall into?

For militaries and governments around the world, the introduction of new technologies to the battlefield should be viewed as a fundamental shift in military conduct and world affairs. What was considered an act of war in the past will differ in the coming years. This presents an even more complicated question that has no answer.

If using technology is the main way military operations are conducted in the future, and technology is not held accountable for its actions, then what, exactly, will start the next war?

Chapter 6

Technological Terrorism
What is the future of terrorism?

September 11, 2031
San Francisco, California

It's 1:30 p.m. on the 30-year anniversary of the 9/11 attacks in the United States. Five cars, driving in different parts of San Francisco, suddenly stop. The cars, which are self-driving, have no ignition key or manual start. The drivers are left waiting, hoping the cars will resume their normal functions.

Three minutes later, the cars turn on and begin moving. They drive off the road and onto sidewalks as the drivers panic and try to take control. The cars accelerate toward groups of people, running them over at deadly speeds.

At this point, more than 50 people have died.

The cars continue their rampage. More people are run over and killed, while others are badly injured by being struck as they jump out of the way — an employee on a lunch break, a mother walking with her young daughter, a student waiting for a bus, all are affected.

The drivers are in shock. Unable to stop the cars or to jump out, they're forced to watch the destruction their vehicles are creating.

After 20 minutes, the vehicles stop. The doors unlock. More than 200 people have been killed, and hundreds more are injured. None of the drivers, victims, or bystanders can comprehend that a terrorist attack has just taken place.

Introduction

Terrorism is wreaking havoc around the world. While 9/11 remains the most well-known terrorist attack, countless others have taken place, before and since 9/11, that show just how serious a threat terrorism poses to the world.

In 1972, a Palestinian terrorist group called Black September took hostage eleven members of the Israeli Olympic team during the 1972 Summer Olympics in Munich, Germany. All hostages were killed.

In June 1985, Sikh terrorists demanding an independent Punjab state in India detonated a bomb on an Air India plane. It had been flying from Montreal to London and New Delhi. The plane plunged into the Atlantic Ocean, and all 329 people on board were killed.

In December 2001, terrorists affiliated with the Lashkar-e-Taiba and Jaish-e-Mohammed groups used fake stickers and badges to enter the Indian Parliament. Using their vehicle, they rammed the car of the Indian vice president, exited the vehicle, and started shooting.

On September 21, 2013, gunmen stormed a shopping mall in Nairobi, Kenya, and began attacking innocent civilians. Sixty-seven people died, and another 175 were wounded. The Muslim terrorist group Al-Shabaab claimed responsibility.

In today's world, terrorism has become a frequent phenomenon. Attacks are being carried out weekly: a beheading in the United Kingdom, a hostage crisis in Bangladesh, a bomb blast in Turkey. The world is struggling to keep up with this new, radical wave of terror. As governments struggle to deal with the current terrorism challenge, they could be overlooking something equally important: the future of terrorism.

The future of terrorism is not so much about who will be the future terrorists, or what their demands might be. The more pressing issue is what methods terrorists will use in the future to incite chaos.

Today, terrorists utilize bombs, guns, suicide vests, and more. Tomorrow, could these same terrorists take advantage of self-driving cars, heavy-lifting drones, advanced cyber attacks, and more?

Self-Driving Cars

In July 2014, the US Federal Bureau of Investigation (FBI) released an unclassified report that looked at the risk self-driving cars create for law-enforcement — specifically in the way crimes are carried out. The FBI took this one step further. They included the terrorist element in the analysis, and said self-driving cars could be used as lethal weapons.[132]

In March 2016 — more than two years after the FBI's report on self-driving cars — a U.S. cyber-security expert said there's evidence of the Islamic State of Iraq and Syria (ISIS) working on self-driving cars to use them to deliver attacks.[133] In fact, a video shows members of Jihadi University hacking certain parts of vehicles, like the steering wheel, to enable them to be controlled remotely.[134] Is the groundwork already being laid down for self-driving cars to be used in terrorist attacks?

Today, experts can hack into cars to enable them to be remote-controlled. This was showcased in 2015 in a *WIRED* article that described a journalist in an SUV being manipulated by two hackers, to show what is possible.[135] Tomorrow, as self-driving cars become a popular means of transport, terrorists could use cyber attacks instead of physically hacking into the vehicles.

The Islamic State (IS) already has a cyber army — called the Caliphate Cyber Army (CCA) — working in support of such attacks. In the future, CCA or another pro-IS hacking group could launch cyber attacks against security networks designed to protect self-driving cars from external control or other tampering. After breaking into these networks, the hackers could gain control of vehicles and make them execute a number of attacks — such as driving onto sidewalks in the middle of the day, rampaging through parks where kids are playing — causing collisions on a massive scale.

The possibility of IS hackers causing collisions between self-driving cars could also be used as a diversion to keep emergency responders too busy to stop a larger, simultaneous attack.

Under this scenario of future terrorism, a new obstacle emerges when it comes to protecting people. Does the responsibility of protecting self-driving cars from being hacked by terrorists lie with the government or the automaker? Should the responsibility lie with both parties? Also, how will consumer privacy be affected?[136]

Drones

After the 9/11 attacks, one of the biggest questions authorities and investigators asked was how the terrorists managed to get on the planes and gain command of them. This line of thinking has influenced airport security policies and terrorist-identification methods. The logic is, if you can stop a terrorist before she or he gets on a plane, no damage can be done. One technology changes this logic and calculation: drones.

A professor at the University of Birmingham in the United Kingdom said in 2014 that terrorists could use drones to bring down planes by crashing the drones into the planes' engines.[137] His comments came after a near hit and miss between a drone and an Airbus A320 that had been landing at Heathrow Airport. The drone came within twenty feet of the plane.[138]

Consumer drones are easy to purchase. If purchased in bulk, they could create an unprecedented amount of chaos for countries around the world. A future terrorist attack could see terrorists remotely controlling dozens of drones and ramming them into planes, with a goal of causing plane crashes and killing everyone on board.

Today, few defenses exist to stop drones. In fact, some companies even allow users to turn off geofencing, a technology that creates virtual barriers, stopping the drone from going into certain areas.[139]

One kind of defense against drones is emerging in the United States. At select airports, the Federal Aviation Administration (FAA) is testing out a system to contend with unmanned aerial vehicles (UAVs). Its Anti-UAV Defense System (AUDS) can identify threats up to six miles away. Once a threat is identified, AUDS sends out a beam to jam the signals a drone receives.[140]

If AUDS is installed at La Guardia Airport in New York, and terrorists try to send in drones to ram the engines of planes landing or taking off, AUDS sends out a signal to scramble the signal the drones are receiving. This will render them unable to move in the way the operator (terrorist) desires.

Another defense is to train local wildlife. In 2016, police in the Netherlands partnered with a bird-training company to find out whether it's possible to train eagles to take down drones.[141]

Here's the problem: AUDS or eagles would be able to protect against drones only in certain settings, such as in a city or airport. Planes, however, spend most of their time 20,000 or 30,000 feet in the air outside cities and airports. As drones advance, so will their altitude and flight-time capabilities.

Many airports, in compliance with the airspace regulations of their countries, require planes to lower their altitude 30 to 40 minutes before landing. Is this an opportunity for terrorists to launch attacks against incoming planes using the advanced drones of tomorrow?

One strategy to protect against drone-terrorist attacks is for planes to install AUDS-type systems on board. As in the example of self-driving cars, however, whose responsibility is this — the airlines or the governments?

Attacking planes is just one way terrorists could utilize drones. Another way would be to attack important people or populated venues.

While U.S. President Barack Obama was vacationing in Hawaii in late 2015, a drone moved into close proximity of his motorcade. Secret Service officials jumped into action and identified who was controlling the drone. Luckily, it was an innocent accident, and the owner complied with the requests of the authorities.[142]

The drone could have been carrying an explosive device, or it could have been used to gather data on Secret Service reaction times.

This incident signifies something else. If drones can move into close proximity of the most powerful and well-protected people on Earth, every person and venue is fair game for future drone terrorism. A British think tank warned of this risk in 2016, saying " ... drones will be used as simple, affordable, and effective airborne improvised explosive devices ... ."[143]

Today, music concerts are popular. Thousands of people pack into a stadium, hall, or park. Is this an opportunity for terrorists? Could they install bombs on drones and ram them into crowds at concerts, killing hundreds, if not thousands, of people? What about malls, outdoor sport games, apartment buildings, and other crowded places?

When it comes to drone terrorism, this risk becomes even more complicated when one integrates other technologies — like mind control.

An April 2016 competition at Florida University involved sixteen pilots controlling and racing drones with their minds. Pilots wore an electroencephalography (EEG) headset, which sells for approximately US$500. These EEG headsets monitored the brain signals of each pilot by tracking where the pilot's neurons fired in relation to where the pilot wanted the drone to move. The EEG headset then converted this signal into a command and sent it to the drone.[144] The professor that organized the competition wants "brain-drone racing teams" to be ready by 2017.

What does this mean for future terrorism?

Currently, drones require an operator to be in proximity to them. When it comes to drones attacking concerts, theoretically, authorities may be able to track the operator of the drone because that person must be near the concert venue.

With mind-control technology, this changes. As this drone mind-control technology advances, a person could control a drone from thousands of miles away. This could also change how and where to jail terrorists and suspects — or whether to jail them at all.

Islamic extremists in Somalia could conduct multiple terrorist attacks on Shanghai, New Delhi, and Moscow by using mind-controlled drones, delivering them accurately wherever they wanted, without ever leaving their home base. Would this be called drone "suicide attacks"?

Governments may not be ready for this level of sophistication when it comes to future terrorism. This leaves populations exposed.

Smart Everything

Appliances and devices today are marketed based on one major theme: connectivity. Whether it's a smart dishwasher, a smart thermostat, or a smart stove, appliances are now connected to the Internet and can be remote-controlled through a smartphone app.

General Electric (GE) unveiled a new line of appliances called Profile Series in 2015. These sophisticated appliances can be controlled via a smartphone. The GE oven can be preheated using the app, the fridge can let its owner know if the door has been left open, and the washer can tell you when the clothes are finished.[145]

For most people, this connectivity provides a new kind of communication with the appliances we use every day. For those with more nefarious goals, smart appliances and their internet connectivity present a new opportunity to create chaos.

Take, for instance, the smart thermostat, like the one Nest sells. At Black Hat USA 2014, researchers hacked a Nest thermostat during a demonstration, and manipulated the message the device showed.

At that time, the only way to hack the device was to have physical access to it. The fear was that a hacker could buy the Nest thermostat in bulk, install a virus in the thermostats, and then resell them on eBay or other Internet sales platforms. Buyers would unknowingly give this hacker access to their personal information.[146]

During the same conference, researchers said they were already working on hacking the Nest device remotely.

As hackers gain even more sophisticated tools, will terrorist hackers be able to break into smart devices and manipulate them in dangerous ways?

By 2020, tens of billions of devices will be connected to the Internet — known as the "Internet of Things."[147] As more and more people purchase connected devices, such as smart appliances, they could unknowingly make themselves vulnerable to dangerous situations.

In the future, terrorists could hack into a Nest thermostat or another smart thermostat. Many of these thermostats have an "away" feature for use when the owner is not at home. This feature would give terrorists knowledge of when to strike. When the owner is not at home, terrorists could program the heat to a very high temperature. They could also hack into a smart oven and smart stove and turn them on, all at maximum heat settings. The result: A fire starts in a home due to three smart devices.

This may sound unimaginable to many of us, because our appliances aren't smart. In the future, home buyers may only have access to smart appliances. These appliances will gain even more capabilities and features around connectivity and remote control.

How will law enforcement react to dozens of calls reporting that a stove has caught fire? How will a country react when an investigation concludes that the source of the fires was a terrorist attack through cyber means?

Like the examples with self-driving cars and drones, the question arises of where the responsibility lies when it comes to terrorism through smart appliances — with the manufacturer or the government?

Conclusion

Today, the risks of terrorism are clear. They're in the shape of bombs, guns, suicide vests, and more. For the most part, we are able to identify the terrorist organizations — Al Qaeda, Al Nusra, ISIS/Islamic State of Iraq and the Levant (ISIL), Al-Shabaab, and Boko Haram, to name a few.

As new technologies advance, such as self-driving cars, drones, and connected appliances, new ways to create chaos will also emerge. Terrorists are already exploring some of these technologies, as in the case of self-driving cars. When the methods of delivery increase, so too will the number and type of terrorists.

We may see the rise of digital terrorists, who specialize in utilizing new technologies to conduct attacks. These terrorists could be scattered across the globe, operate only occasionally, and use communication channels in the Deep Web to talk and plan. Are countries ready for terrorism from these kinds of groups?

One of the most pressing issues is around responsibility and response.

First, who is responsible for protecting the items consumers buy — the manufacturer or the government? This hasn't been an issue before, because counterterrorism was — and still is — mainly about restricting terrorist movements. If terrorists are not moving in the conventional way and are instead taking advantage of the products that companies sell, however, it blurs the lines of responsibility and changes how governments and intelligence agencies will have to approach terrorism in the future.

Second, how will governments respond? After 9/11, the United States had a clear culprit: Al Qaeda. Officials in the United States knew Al Qaeda had a stronghold in Afghanistan, which led to the U.S. war in Afghanistan. Tomorrow, if a digital-terrorist group hacked into self-driving cars throughout Europe and ran over people, at whom European governments point a finger, and how would their militaries respond, if at all?

All these questions point to the shifting nature of terrorism as new technologies make their way into the world. Many of these technologies, and the products that have emerged or will emerge from them, will provide tremendous benefits and advantages to the people using them.

At the same time, they carry a new kind of risk. Those who want to incite chaos could utilize these technologies and products to meet radical goals. As governments all over the world prepare for the terrorist threats of today, are they overlooking what's on the horizon?

Chapter 7

Drone Dependency
Are countries becoming technologically handicapped?

Kigali, Rwanda
October 2030-33

In 2030, Rwanda launched a free, state-of-the-art drone program that covered the entire country, with a special focus on rural areas. The system is preprogrammed to have drones pick up certain goods every day — blood supplies, food rations, fresh water, vaccines, and more — and drop them off to communities all over the nation. It's part of a government program to raise the quality of life for people, and to reduce disease.

In 2032, an insurgency problem emerged in Rwanda. A group by the name of Free Rwanda Guerrillas (FRG) began setting off bombs at power grids and drone-charging ports to stop the program. They claim the government is putting Rwanda into debt and giving control of the country to international lenders to fund the drone program.

The FRG took a new approach at the start of 2033. They began launching advanced cyber attacks against the government drones, jamming their signals and making them crash to the ground. After months of this, the rural populations dependent on the drones' deliveries of basic supplies began to protest against the government and FRG. Ethnic tensions resurfaced, and the government struggled to find a proper solution.

For decades, the government relied on drones to improve the conditions of the people in their country. In the process, they neglected building and repairing roads and highways.

Now, there's is no way to send basic supplies to these rural communities in a reliable way. Anger is spreading.

Introduction

For thousands of years, the world has been divided into countries that are developed and those that are developing — first world versus third world. First-world countries, like the United States, Germany, and France, seem to have a bigger say in world affairs than third-world countries.

The criteria that governments, institutions, and people have used to define whether a country is developed or developing have not changed in recent years. Does the country have basic physical infrastructure, such as reliable, efficient, and safe road networks; power grids; and sanitation systems? Can a majority of people access services such as healthcare, education, and emergency responders? Is the political, economic, and social environment within the country stable and sustainable?

Countries that are developing have sought to develop and reach the same level as the so-called developed, advanced world. This has been tough. The high costs involved mean that many countries have to borrow from international lenders in unfair ways. Political and social challenges also present themselves. Many developing countries suffer from dirty politics and an almost permanent presence of corruption. Equally important is the geopolitical strategy of other countries to limit and restrict certain countries and regions from advancing.

The criteria that has labelled countries and structured the world is now falling apart. New technologies allow countries to move past development hurdles, fueling what is called leapfrog development. An example of leapfrog development can be seen in the different ways people access the Internet in the developed world as opposed to the developing world. In the developed world, many people first accessed the Internet through a computer (desktop or laptop) or a cell phone, progressing to a smartphone and now a tablet. In the developing world, people are skipping all these phases and accessing the Internet for the first time with their smartphones. In fact, many of these people may not own computers at all.

As countries take advantage of new technologies to leapfrog past developmental handicaps, they may not invest in traditional methods of development, such as building an advanced network of roads and highways. By not investing in traditional methods, these countries and their populations are at risk of becoming dependent on the technologies they deploy to develop. What happens tomorrow when a technology stops working and people are dependent on it for their livelihood?

Drone Dependency

Drones are unmanned robotic machines whose capabilities determine the ability to navigate different terrains, such as air, land or sea. Drones fall into several categories with the two most important being military drones and consumer drones.

Military drones are highly advanced and autonomous. Classified as UAVs, the drones can be remote-controlled by soldiers on the battlefield or from thousands of miles away in a base, for different purposes. An example of military UAVs are the Predator drones the United States uses to conduct strikes against terrorists around the world. The United States has used Predator drones to conduct strikes in several countries, including Pakistan, Yemen, and Somalia.

Consumer drones aren't used to conduct strikes against terrorists. Instead, they're fitted with cameras that allow people to take pictures and record videos in different settings on land or in the air. An example of a consumer drone is the Parrot Bebop 2. Using four propellers, it's capable of traveling at 37 miles per hour, and staying in the air for twenty-five minutes. It can be controlled via a smartphone.[148]

Along with military and consumer drones, companies are creating drones to solve specific problems. For example, GE uses drones to ensure that power grids are functioning properly,[149] while Facebook is looking to drones to deliver Internet service.[150]

When it comes to countries using drones in a nonmilitary way, Africa stands apart from the rest of the world. Malawi, a landlocked country in southeastern Africa, partnered in 2016 with UNICEF in a trial using drones for

HIV testing. The objective was to reduce the wait time for testing blood samples, which can take up to ten weeks. With drones, the wait time could be brought down to mere days.[151]

Police in Cape Town, South Africa, performed a test using drones during a drug bust in 2015. A drone was deployed in the air above the drug bust scene. It was tasked with tracking suspects that tried to run away or hide drugs and weapons.[152]

In 2014, a $103 million project began in Kenya to stop illegal poaching. The Kenyan government deployed drones to all its national parks and reserves. The drones used radio frequencies to scan the land, as well as animal movements, to identify poachers before they struck.[153]

Rwanda's Drone Vision

If Africa is the hotbed of drone advancement, Rwanda is Africa's hotbed of using drones to pursue leapfrog development. Rwanda was selected in 2015 to be part of a drone-delivery project. If approved, three drone ports would be set for construction in 2016, expected for completion in 2020. Initially, the drones would deliver payloads weighing a total of 10 kilograms. By 2025, payloads of 100 kilograms would be possible.[154]

Rwanda partnered in 2016 with Zipline, a US robotics company, to set up an autonomous system for delivering healthcare to rural parts of the country. Drones will be used to deliver blood supplies and other healthcare needs.[155] Also stepping into the project is UPS, which committed $800,000 toward using drones in the delivery of blood transfusions and vaccines in Rwanda.[156]

Rwanda is investing to create an advanced drone infrastructure in the country, capable of delivering a range of goods, such as health-related supplies, to those who need them. The country's goal with this investment is to develop rapidly.

Rwanda lacks proper road infrastructure. Beyond main roads, the rest of the roads in the country — many of them called feeder lines — are in bad shape due to the war. And even if new roads are built, lighting is needed. In Rwanda, electricity costs can be three to four times higher than in neighboring countries.[157] In addition, 63 percent of people in Rwanda live below the poverty line, and 44.3 percent of children under age 5 suffer from stunting.[158]

For Rwanda, drones provide the ability to fast-track development. The country won't have to invest billions of dollars in roads and highways to connect the country to the people. Drones, which are a lot cheaper, can be used to provide some of the same benefits that roads

offer. By delivering basic healthcare supplies —
and in the future, perhaps food, fresh water,
petrol, and more — Rwanda can develop and
raise the quality of life for its citizens.

While drones are an inexpensive and
superior solution to assist development in the
short term, they also have long-term risks for a
country like Rwanda. Because Rwanda's
population is largely rural — with 73 percent, or
approximately 6,789,000 people, living in rural
areas — and the country has poor road
infrastructure, drones could become the only
way to access basic supplies in a cheap and
reliable way for most of the population. These
rural populations, which may not have the
money or capability (transport) to purchase
basic supplies, could grow dependent on the
government's drone deliveries.

If these drone deliveries stop tomorrow
due to a cyber attack or lack of government
funding, rural populations will be at risk of
losing a supply line on which they've become
dependent. In other words, these populations
will have become drone dependent. If only 5
percent of Rwanda's rural population becomes
drone dependent, that's 339,450 people.

What does drone dependency mean for a
country? One consequence is potential unrest. In
the past, when populations have lost access to
basic supplies, it has fueled migration and
violence. An example of this is Syria, which as

of July 2016, is engulfed in a bloody civil war that began in 2011. Today, this civil war is fueled by religion and ideology. One of the main causes of the Syrian Civil War, however, had nothing to do with religion or ideology. It had everything to do with people losing access to a steady supply of fresh water.

Between 2006 and 2011, one of the worst droughts in history hit Syria. With vital water supplies vanishing, hundreds of thousands of people began to migrate to Aleppo and other parts of the country. This migration, which caused social, political, and economic shockwaves, is viewed as one of the main reasons for the current civil war.[159]

Is there a connection here? Will Rwanda's rural populations face the same risks that Syria's population did before the drought hit? If the drone deliveries of essential supplies stop tomorrow, what will these rural populations do? This question becomes even more important if the government has not constructed an alternative means of delivering these basic supplies into rural areas, such as roads and highways. Loss of supplies can push these drone-dependent populations into dangerous situations.

In Rwanda, rural populations that have become drone dependent and lose basic supplies may migrate elsewhere, like people in Syria did when they moved near Aleppo. Cities in

Rwanda, like Kigali, Butare, or Gitarama are all possible destinations for these drone migrants. This means tens of thousands of people may arrive in a city that is unprepared for this migration. Just as in Aleppo, these cities may face economic, social, and political shockwaves as people from different ethnicities and socioeconomic groups are forced to live together.

The second possibility is that these drone-dependent populations may grow angry and begin revolting. A lack of supplies has been responsible for violent protests in the past. What will these populations do? In 2016, protests began in India over jobs. A caste group got angry at the government over job quotas, and seized control of a water canal. As a result, 10 million people lost water in New Delhi.[160]

Will rural populations in Rwanda storm power facilities and disrupt power supplies, or challenge the government and create their own separate states with their own rules? Either way, the government in Rwanda may not have planned for a situation in which their drones stop operating — and the resulting social and political challenges.

The New Geopolitical Risk

Countries implementing drones and other new technologies to engage in leapfrog development should consider the geopolitical risks that come with them.

First, if a country is using a technology to develop, what are they using the technology instead of? In the case of Rwanda, the government is, perhaps without realizing it, using drones instead of building a system of roads and highways on par with what exists in the developed world.

When a country is developing and using technology as an alternative to something else, it can become a risk. In the future, if this technology stops working, it will have an immediate effect on populations that depend on it.

Second, will countries use drone exports as a way to limit the development of other countries? If drones are used by dozens of countries around the world to leapfrog forward, it could fuel development at a rate that other powers may not like or want. Allowing or curtailing drone exports may be used to either allow for development or hinder it.

Third, will neighboring countries intercept these drones and steal the goods they carry? Rwanda borders on the Democratic Republic of Congo and Burundi. These countries could decide to intercept drones and steal the fresh water, food, fuel, or other goods they carry. How would Rwanda respond?

Fourth, will drone deliveries and other such technologies change the migratory patterns of people? One of the reasons for urbanization is that cities give people more access to goods. If these goods can be accessed by rural populations, will they choose to leave their area?

Finally, why are governments choosing to adopt drone technologies over more traditional solutions? Usually, the main reason is cost. For Rwanda, it's far cheaper to purchase fleets of drones and program them to deliver supplies than it is to build an advanced network of roads and highways.

Cost may be only a temporary setback. Today, the traditional route is expensive. In the future, will it be cheaper? Tomorrow, if Rwanda is able to 3D print the materials for roads and use drones to move road parts into place, will countries still rely on drones for delivering supplies, or will they pursue building traditional infrastructure using new methods?

Conclusion

Countries around the world are looking to new technologies as a way to leapfrog forward and rapidly develop. The benefits are clear. The risks are being overlooked.

Alongside delivering basic supplies like blood and vaccines, developing countries can use them to deal with terrorism (surveillance), fuel the economy through advanced logistics (drone deliveries for e-commerce), and offer a new form of emergency responders (drone firefighters or ambulances).

Each use presents its own set of challenges and risks. An equally important challenge is the way we measure how developed or underdeveloped a country is in this era of new technologies.

Is Rwanda still a developing country in terms of infrastructure if its drone-delivery network is more efficient and reliable than the road system in Portugal? If Brazil begins to manage its entire tax system using artificial intelligence, will it be considered more advanced than Germany, which may still be using electronic or paper filing?

New technologies allow countries to develop in ways, and at a pace, the world has never before experienced. For many countries, this developmental capability will outweigh any perceived risks. For others, developing a contingency plan in the event a technology breaks down is critical.

These technologies will redefine how we measure the importance of countries. In the future, countries may be defined based on the capabilities of their drones, artificial intelligence, and robotics. The countries that excel in these areas may not be the traditional powers.

Are countries ready to operate in a world like this?

Chapter 8

Predictive Foreign Policy
How will countries use artificial intelligence?

Moscow, Russia
2035-2038

The Armed Forces of the Russian Federation developed and deployed a new artificial intelligence system in 2035 to counter future threats. Based in St. Petersburg, the system differs from previous systems Russia has deployed. This new artificial intelligence system was created with one goal in mind: to predict what countries may do, with near-perfect accuracy.

At the beginning of 2035, the artificial intelligence system made its first prediction: In July 2036, the United States and Mexico would go to war over disputed territory. The artificial intelligence system was right in every respect except one: The war took place in January 2036 — months before the prediction.

In March 2037, the artificial intelligence made a second prediction — this time directly affecting Russia. It predicted that by 2038, China would launch an attack to reclaim parts of Outer Manchuria, currently part of Russia. Alarmed by this, Russian officials are forced to act. But how do they respond?

Introduction

Think about every event in the history of mankind that led to a war. What would be the outcome if countries knew in advance, with great accuracy, what was going to happen?

One of the main causes of World War I was the assassination of Archduke Franz Ferdinand by a Serbian militant group called the Black Hand. This caused the Austro-Hungarian Empire to declare war on Serbia. Due to treaties, Germany later declared war on France and invaded Belgium.

What if France and Belgium knew in advance what Germany's choices would be, and took pre-emptive action? What if Germany knew in advance how France, Belgium, and other European powers would respond to an invasion, allowing German forces to change their strategy?

Decades later, World War II began. The formal beginning was the German invasion of Poland. What if European powers knew of

Hitler's plans in advance? How would the Japanese Empire have changed its strategy with the knowledge that an attack on Pearl Harbor in the United States would result in an atomic response?

Apply this same logic to the Cold War, Vietnam War, Korean War, Indo-Pakistani War, the ongoing wars in Afghanistan and Iraq, the Syrian War, the Libyan War, and others. How would the outcomes change if the warring parties could predict events before they took place? With this kind of foresight, history may have taken an alternative route, and the world as we know it could be very different. Before, the means of prediction were out of reach. Going forward, they won't be.

Artificial intelligence is rapidly advancing. It's defined as the "... power of a machine to copy intelligent human behavior ... ."[161] This is, arguably, a conservative definition. Artificial intelligence will not only be able to copy intelligent human behavior, it will be able to surpass it in all kinds of ways. Why? Government-backed artificial intelligence will have access to all the data in the world, on a scale that human beings cannot process.

In 1992, the world was producing 100 gigabytes of data every day. By 2002, the world was producing 100 gigabytes of data every second. By 2018, this figure is projected to reach 50,000 gigabytes. As of 2015, 90 percent of all the data in the world was created in the past two years.[162]

Here's another way to look at it: Every sixty seconds, seventy-two hours of video are uploaded on YouTube, 278,000 Tweets are sent out on Twitter, two million search queries are processed by Google, 571 new websites are created, and 3,600 photos are shared on Instagram. One can even look past the sixty-second interval. On Facebook, 41,000 posts take place every second.[163]

Within all this data — which also include emails, phone calls, and text messages — lie powerful patterns, trends, and predictions. The more data to which artificial intelligence has access, the faster it can learn and eventually predict what may take place in the future. This predictive capability can be deployed by governments for a variety of purposes, including to determine what will take place in world affairs and beyond. This foresight carries new risks. How will countries behave when they can predict one another's actions and more?

Prediction Means Pre-Emptive?

The ability to predict events is being pursued around the world.

Russia's Federal Agency for Ethnic Affairs unveiled a new capability in early 2016, announcing the development of software that uses artificial intelligence to detect early-stage ethnic conflicts in the country.[164] In other words, Russia would be able to predict a separatist movement in Chechnya before it spreads — or begins.

In China, Baidu — the Chinese version of Google — has developed an algorithm that can predict where crowds will form by using data from Baidu Maps. It can be used by the government to stop crowds perceived as dangerous, and deploy police.[165]

Alongside developments in Russia and China, India announced in 2016 that it's developing a supercomputer to predict future monsoons. The entire project will cost $60 million, and if the predictions are accurate, it could give farmers the information to increase yields by 15 percent.[166]

These developments represent some of the first steps toward countries having the capability to predict events. Once countries gain this ability, they may deploy it to predict the actions of another country.

In 2012, a pro-government newspaper in China called *Wen Weipo* published an article entitled, "Six Wars China Is Sure to Fight in the Next 50 Years." The article touched on all areas where China is experiencing regional tension, including Taiwan, Japan, and India. The last of the six war predictions was titled, "Recover the Territory Seized by Russia," which is projected to take place between 2050 and 2060. The territories seized by Russia refer to Outer Manchuria, which was once a part of China but is now under Russian control.

Today, a military conflict between Russia and China appears unthinkable. Both countries are working together in many areas. They've signed mammoth energy deals. In 2014, Russia and China signed a natural gas deal worth $400 billion.[167] Months later, both countries signed a second natural gas deal, making Russia the supplier for one-fifth of all natural gas that China imports.[168]

They're also taking their geopolitical partnership beyond energy. In June 2016, a Chinese frigate moved in proximity to the disputed Senkaku/Diaoyu Islands in the South China Sea, past the 12-mile boundary. These are islands that China and Japan dispute, with Japan claiming sovereignty over them. Japanese media reported that during China's incursion, three Russian military vessels were spotted in the same area.[169] Coincidence or cooperation?

Today's relationship between Russia and China should not overlook the reality of the changing world environment. Today, Russian and Chinese interests converge. Tomorrow, Russian and Chinese interests could collide.

An area where this is likely is Central Asia. China is investing heavily in this region as part of its New Silk Road initiative. Russia, however, considers Central Asia part of its sphere of influence. If Central Asia becomes the catalyst for China–Russia tensions, these tensions could expand into other areas, such as territorial sovereignty.

As the scenario at the beginning of the chapter suggests, if Russia were to deploy artificial-intelligence software in the future and was alerted that China would soon launch an attack to retake parts of Outer Manchuria, how would Russia respond? Such a prediction would place Russia in a tricky and dangerous situation. Russia could not ignore the prediction. It would be forced to act — but in what capacity? Each action carries a risk.

Russia could increase surveillance over Outer Manchuria and parts of China, but this would risk alerting China to Russia's awareness of the impending attack. Or Russia could deploy troops and military assets to the disputed territory, but this could create the conditions for a violent conflict.

Russia also has a third option at its disposal: pre-emptive action.

This is one of the main risks predictive foreign policy brings to world affairs. It can increase the likelihood that countries will take pre-emptive action to prevent the events predicted by the artificial intelligence.

In the 2030s, pre-emptive action from Russia could take several forms. Russia could launch a sustained cyber-attack campaign to crash Chinese power grids, Internet communications, and stock exchanges. Russia could also use nanotechnology to bring a new kind of warfare to the Chinese population. Finally, in the least likely and most dangerous scenario, Russia could decide to attack China first, bombing air fields, major cities, and missile bases. Any choice pits Russia and China against each other.

More importantly, all Russia's choices stem from a prediction made by artificial intelligence.

Artificial Intelligence Race

The ability to predict events will not be confined to one country. Several countries will have it.

In the United States, DARPA is leading the advancement of America's artificial-intelligence capabilities.[170] In February 2016, DARPA unveiled two key projects that shed light on the growing artificial-intelligence capabilities the United States will possess in the coming years. First, DARPA said it was working on an artificial-intelligence program to create on-demand jamming frequencies for fighter jets. Currently, jamming frequencies are preprogrammed. If the planes using these frequencies experience a signal they haven't seen before, they're left unprotected. Under its new program, DARPA seeks to remove this risk from the battlefield by using artificial intelligence to update the frequencies in real time.[171] In the same month, DARPA unveiled a project for a microchip called Eyeriss that is tiny enough to be installed in mobile devices and has 168 cores (smartphones have only four cores). Eyeriss is modeled after the brain's neural network, and has artificial intelligence installed in it. The plan is for DARPA to use the Eyeriss microchip to give drones and robots autonomous capabilities on the battlefield.[172]

If DARPA is developing these capabilities today, what will their artificial-intelligence capabilities be by 2030?

South Korea is also an emerging artificial-intelligence power. After Google's DeepMind (AlphaGo) defeated a South Korean player in the ancient Chinese game "GO" in 2016, South Korea was left in a state of shame. To ensure South Korea becomes an artificial-intelligence leader, the government in Seoul earmarked $3.4 billion in March 2016 to fuel artificial-intelligence projects in the public and private sectors.[173] One such project is called Exobrain, the goal of which is to take on IBM Watson, an artificial-intelligence computer system from the United States.[174]

With multiple countries investing in artificial intelligence, it's likely that in the future, we'll witness artificial intelligence from different countries competing with one another. From a geopolitical standpoint, this could start off with multiple countries predicting what others will do. Russia may predict a Chinese invasion, China may predict a Russian awareness, while South Korea may predict a China–Russia war in Asia, and so forth. With each progressive prediction, the strategies of the country will change, and most likely, the artificial intelligence will take this into account, updating its prediction.

On the sidelines, other countries with predictive artificial intelligence deployed will gauge their own geopolitical strategies. The United States may predict a Russia–China war. Perhaps America's artificial intelligence would alert it to the role the United States would play in such a conflict. Maybe the United States would use its artificial intelligence to predict the outcomes of different strategies it could use during a Russia–China war.

Predictive artificial intelligence will give countries the ability to know what's coming.

The capabilities behind predictive artificial intelligence can also be used by countries in other ways — like with foreign direct investment (FDI). A country's FDI is used to gauge how attractive or unattractive it is for businesses and governments. For example, in 2015 India became the world's economic superstar, simultaneously leading world economic growth and receiving $63 billion in FDI, overtaking China as the world's top destination for foreign investment.[175]

Today, countries use traditional methods to decide where to invest. This includes a mixture of examining indexes, economic models, and projections; and assessing market conditions, existing debt, interest-rate changes, currency volatility, and more.

Tomorrow, instead of software and a group of humans deciding where to invest, a country could create an artificial-intelligence fund to manage its foreign direct investment. In fact, funds managed by artificial intelligence aren't a theory, they're real. A Hong Kong-based hedge fund called Aidyia launched an artificial intelligence–based trading system in January 2016. It crunches data and makes trades—sometimes with suggestions from other artificial-intelligence engines. On its first day, its trades resulted in a 2 percent return.[176]

A banker in Japan developed an artificial-intelligence system in 2016 that uses algorithms to forecast future stock market conditions. Deployed between 2012 and 2016, the system was right thirty-two of forty-seven times.[177] Could the Japanese government build on this technology and develop an artificial-intelligence fund to handle FDI?

Japan could set parameters on its artificial-intelligence fund, such as where it can invest (eg, only outside Japan) and how much it can spend (eg, a maximum investment of $1 billion). Within these parameters, Japan's artificial-intelligence fund would start looking for investments. India could be selected. After approval from Tokyo, Japan's artificial-intelligence fund could begin investing in India.

The artificial-intelligence fund will invest differently than a human investor. Human investors have biases, rules, bosses, emotions, and other features unique to humans. Artificial intelligence doesn't. The artificial-intelligence fund could simultaneously invest in the Indian stock market, government bonds, loans in micro-finance, startup funding, insurance, and more.

As Japan's artificial-intelligence fund penetrates the Indian economy, India could decide to develop its own artificial-intelligence fund for FDI, and deploy it in Japan. Then, artificial-intelligence funds from two separate countries would be competing with each other to protect their home markets and return the most money.

If either fund was successful in its first few years of operation, Japan or India could unleash the full potential of its artificial intelligence — removing parameters, such as how much money the fund can invest. This would mean the artificial-intelligence fund could invest $2 billion or $5 billion — or take a loan.

What would happen if Japan's fund were to invest in stocks throughout the Indian economy, then pull out so much money that it damaged the Indian economy? What would this mean for Japan–India relations if a Japanese artificial-intelligence fund was responsible for economic damage in India?

An equally important concern is how countries would respond to an artificial-intelligence fund from another country investing across the board. Some countries could see this as a risk to national security — too much foreign influence and control. This is what happened in May 2016, when Midea, a Chinese appliance maker, put forward a €4.5bn bid for Kuka, a German robotics company. The European Union and German government began to worry about the effect a Chinese takeover would have on Germany's economic strategy for automation, called Industry 4.0.[178] How would Europe and the world have responded if this bid was made by a Chinese artificial-intelligence fund?

Artificial-intelligence funds deployed by countries or companies to manage investments aren't decades away — in many cases, they've already arrived. The question is, are governments and markets ready for the kind of change this new way of investing will bring?

Bringing in Science Fiction

Artificial intelligence will be a resource for countries, providing them with a new kind of foresight. But at the same time, artificial intelligence will be an entity in itself. As an entity, artificial intelligence presents its own risks — the kind that Elon Musk, Stephen Hawking, Bill Gates, and others have warned us about.

The artificial intelligence that exists today is not a reflection of true artificial intelligence. Instead, it's a very controlled engine more akin to big data. In the future, artificial intelligence won't have the same kind of control built into it. It has been said that the way it will be deployed puts it in the same category as electricity.[179] In other words, artificial intelligence could be everywhere.

Could artificial intelligence systems from around the world communicate with one another? Could an artificial intelligence system create its own desires?

The risk is that a prediction, like the hypothetical one of Russia predicting a Chinese invasion, could actually be created by an artificial intelligence for its own reasons — like bringing the world into a state of war.

For the first time in human history, we're creating something that's literally designed to match and exceed humans in every possible way. It's imperative that we understand the risks of this kind of technology — both from a state level and a moral level.

In fact, the potential of artificial intelligence is so great that the UN chief information technology officer has said it could be humanity's last innovation. The next innovations could come from artificial intelligence itself.[180]

If artificial intelligence does, in fact, become "conscious" and works toward its own goals — such as bringing the world into a state of war — what options are left for countries? If this is a real risk, should governments restrict the access that artificial intelligence has in certain areas, like nuclear weapons control? Will countries even have a choice regarding what artificial intelligence can and cannot access — especially if it is able to think independently, crack codes, and mask its activity from people?

The risks are real, but every technology has risks. In fact, at every major turn in human history, the world has panicked. At the turn of the millennium, people thought the entire digital backbone of the world would stop working (Y2K). They were wrong.

Are we wrong about the risks from artificial intelligence?

Conclusion

A new era in the way countries manage their foreign policy is on the horizon. In the past, governments looked to the experience and connections people had to improve their foresight and predictive capabilities.

In the future, governments will tap artificial intelligence in multiple ways, including predicting events in world affairs and managing foreign investments. This is just the beginning. Artificial intelligence will also advise governments on how to respond to events, and in what ways.

In fact, governments may deploy artificial intelligence to handle entire situations, like negotiating a free-trade agreement with another country or handling a diplomatic disagreement. Humans would merely carry out instructions from artificial intelligence.[181]

If an outbreak of terrorism was on the horizon in Tanzania, Canada — which has many mining companies in the region — could know days in advance, thanks to a prediction from artificial intelligence. Ottawa could alert Canada's mining companies and its embassy in

142

the country, which could evacuate all personnel and suspend operations at the mining sites.

Canada's artificial intelligence could go one step further, however. It could tell Canada what to do afterwards. Canada's artificial-intelligence system could create on-demand schedules for the mining sites, based on the changing real-time risk of terrorism. At the same time, mining companies would only hire security personnel and contractors from a handful of artificial intelligence–vetted organizations. The result? Minimal affect from the terrorism.

The benefits of predictive artificial intelligence are clear, but so are the risks. Countries will make decisions based on a new kind of paranoia about what's coming. In addition, artificial intelligence itself may evolve and have its own motives.

In an era during which geopolitical competition is increasing, governments will be less likely to look at the risks of using artificial intelligence, instead assessing it based on how much of an advantage it gives them. The result is that geopolitics could become more reactive than proactive. Governments could be on the receiving end of artificial-intelligence predictions, struggling to respond or perhaps, to keep up.

Predictive artificial intelligence and the technology behind it present a new dilemma for countries. Will they use it to gain an advantage while exposing themselves to certain risks? Or will they back away to protect themselves, and end up operating blindly?

Back to the Historian

For the past hour, the virtual historian has been answering your question about technologies and their impact on world affairs over the past fifty years.

You've learned how artificial intelligence provided governments around the world with predictive capabilities. You've learned about space colonization and how it led to geopolitical rivalry, the likes of which the world had never seen before.

When the historian talked about designer babies and how they redefined citizenship, you were caught off guard. You're a designer baby, born in the United States but designed in Japan. Not once did you ever think to question how countries delegated responsibility and handled your healthcare costs, tax payments, and more.

As the virtual historian covered other technologies from food cloning to drone dependency, each technology reinforced a realization in your mind. These technologies and their geopolitical impact didn't just affect a few governments and companies. They affected everyone, from a single college student to the population of an underdeveloped country.

With your virtual reality gear still on and a little bit of energy left, you leave the virtual historian simulation. You sift through the virtual reality apps and select the Great Barrier Reef option. Now you're swimming in the Great Barrier Reef — or what's left of it.

As you swim and explore, the simulation gives you information on the environment you're in. It tells you that in 2030, the Great Barrier Reef became so heated and filled with garbage that practically all aquatic life died or migrated elsewhere by 2035. At the same time, all plant life perished, creating a quiet and still body of seawater that is now used to launch spaceships.

After an hour of exploring, you decide to call it a night.

Slipping off the virtual reality gear, you groggily walk to your bedroom. As you lie down, you look at the simulated landscape your smart walls created to help you fall asleep. Based on your vitals and blood analysis, monitored through your smart bracelet and communicated to your smart walls, a different atmosphere is created for you every night.

Tonight's scenario is a boat drifting along a moonlit river in Brazil's Amazon rainforest. You stare at the boat and remember the information the simulation was sharing with you as you swam through the Great Barrier Reef.

Just as your eyes close, you think of another question for the virtual historian. What effect did climate change have on the world over the past 50 years?

Bonus Chapter

Robotic Soft Power

Introduction

Today, countries have two ways of expanding their geopolitical influence. The first way is through hard power. Countries deploy their militaries, governments, and economies to expand their power around the world. In February 2016, Russia loaned Armenia $200 million (over ten years) to purchase Russian defense equipment.[182] This is an example of Russian hard power. The second way countries expand their geopolitical influence is through soft power. Soft power doesn't revolve around the military or the economy. Soft power is generated through nongovernmental means, such as selling lifestyle or technology services.

Examples of American soft power are Starbucks and Apple. Every time a person in another country enters a Starbucks or Apple Store, they're being introduced to, and influenced by, American lifestyle and American technology.

Another example of soft power is Bollywood, the movie industry of India. The content that Bollywood creates is not only consumed by people in India, but by people all over the world. As people watch Bollywood films and television shows, they're being influenced by Indian culture and history.

Now, a new kind of soft power has emerged: robotics. Countries investing in robotics and leading robotic advancements are also equipping themselves with a new way to expand their influence around the world. What does this mean for world affairs?

What Does Robotic Soft Power Look Like?

If you own a fairly-new HTC smartphone, you have likely heard of Hidi. For those who do not own an HTC phone, Hidi is an app that comes with the smartphone and acts as a voice assistant, similar to Apple's Siri or Google's Now. Hidi, however, is not the product of HTC, a Taiwanese company. Hidi was developed by a Chinese company called Turing Robot.

Turing supplies Hidi to HTC (they were also funded by HTC), along with software for personal robots. As of 2016, Turing was receiving almost one billion search queries every day, with the majority of them coming from Hidi.

Turing announced a new software in June 2016, called Turing OS. It's designed for home robots, and comes with voice and text interfaces so developers can create the perfect solution for the robot.[183]

What does all this mean for robotic soft power? Hidi, software from China, is already being used by hundreds of thousands of people with HTC smartphones around the world. This software is learning about these people, their search habits, desires, thoughts, and personalities. With Turing OS, Chinese software enters the home. Home robots, like vacuum cleaners or kitchen appliances, will run Turing OS to operate and provide functionality to users. Like Hidi, Turing OS will receive commands, learn habits, and evolve based on the user and his or her questions and choices.

All these queries, commands and actions give Turing, and by extension, China, major control over the way people interact with their robotic devices. Turing OS, and future versions of Hidi, could become the software standard for robots, giving people little to no alternative in using anything else.

Turing, and by extension, China, could use this influence in several ways. The company could program its software to work better with other Chinese devices, like a DJI drone or a Baidu car. This would influence users of robots loaded with Turing OS to purchase goods from

Chinese companies instead of Western companies.

Turing could program the robot to speak in the user's native language along with Mandarin, teaching people the Chinese language whenever they ask their robot to do something, even if they don't want to hear it.

Software like Turing OS will also place huge amounts of data into the hands of a Chinese company. Tomorrow, home robots will have video cameras, active microphones, sensors, and more. Even when these robots are not active, they may still be on. People's entire lives — from what they say in their car to how they behave at home — could be recorded, with the data controlled by Turing and other such companies. Will this give China unimaginable access to the lives of people around the world? How could China use this knowledge to formulate government strategies, business plans, and more?

In the future, Turing could input all this data into an artificial-intelligence engine and begin to see patterns in households, neighborhoods, societies, and countries around the world. Are people and governments ready for that kind of foreign access?

Turing isn't alone. The same consequences of Turing OS can be applied to Apple's Siri, Google's Now, and Microsoft's

Cortana. This leads to the second theme of robotic soft power — competition.

Yesterday, companies competed over automobiles, consumer electronics, luxury goods, and more. Tomorrow, robotics will become as competitive as the traditional industries, and one of the main benefits of winning this competition (for a country) will be soft power.

If soft power can expand a country's culture, lifestyle, and influence, it will mean that Turing will not be alone in conquering the global robotics market through advanced software. Companies from the United States, Japan, South Korea, India, and Germany will be able to do the same.

Companies from these countries could all enter one market, like Nigeria, and present their robotic-software solutions to people and companies. While each company would operate under traditional business models (ie, profit, expenses, revenue), the country from which the company originates would look at it through a different lens: soft power.

Conclusion

Most markets today fall under two models. Either one leader dominates — like Apple in the case of smartphones in the United

States — or there are dozens of companies — like VW in India — competing.

These, however, are not the most important markets. The most important markets are the ones that are just taking off — such as humanoid robots. As these new markets take off, world affairs and competition between countries heat up.

Soft power will soon become as important as hard power. As more companies invest in robotics, they'll also be implicitly or explicitly pursuing the benefits of robotic soft power.

The stakes have never been higher. The question is, how extreme will companies and countries be willing to go to win this new soft-power race?

Bonus Chapter

Business-Induced Geopolitics

Introduction

If a war breaks out, oil will hit $250. If "they" attack each other's oil facilities, it could hit $500.[184] Those statements were made as relations between Saudi Arabia and Iran deteriorated in 2016 over Saudi Arabia's execution of a Shiite cleric, and the resulting attack on the Saudi embassy in Tehran.[185]

It reflected an age-old tale when it comes to geopolitics: One government does something; another government doesn't like what that government has done, and tensions rise.

This age-old tale is now a fallacy. Going forward, governments are no longer the only ones in the driver's seat when it comes to geopolitics. Technology companies are there, as well.

SpaceKnow

Until now, one of the best ways to assess the health of the manufacturing sector in an economy was through the Institute for Supply Management (ISM) Manufacturing Index. The ISM surveys more than 300 manufacturing firms and tracks variables like employment, new orders, and inventory.[186] This method is being overturned by an American technology startup called SpaceKnow.

SpaceKnow has created a China Satellite Manufacturing Index (SMI). In short, the SMI processes billions of satellite images of Chinese factories, spanning hundreds of thousands of kilometers and covering more than 6,000 industrial sites, to judge the health of China's manufacturing sector.[187]

Hedge funds and private investors are paying close attention to SpaceKnow's service. One of the main reasons for this is that the economic numbers coming out of China don't reflect the picture on the ground.

As more foreign companies use SpaceKnow's SMI to make decisions, the Chinese government could become angry. One way China could respond is by saying that SpaceKnow breaches China's national security. In 2014, China took steps against American companies over alleged spying. Windows 8 was banned from government computers,[188] state-owned companies were told not to use consulting services from McKinsey,[189] and IBM servers were banned in banks.[190] In the eyes of China, is SpaceKnow spying?

In this case, China can't resort to bans. SpaceKnow doesn't have an office in China. More importantly, their entire operation bypasses China — it's based on data gathered from space. The only way for China to take on SpaceKnow is to take it up directly with the U.S. government.

This creates a new challenge. The U.S. government is being pulled into a geopolitical spat over the innovations of an American company that isn't even operating in China.

SpaceKnow isn't the only one creating this new geopolitical scenario. Facebook is, too.

Facebook

In February 2016, Facebook's Connectivity Lab unveiled an artificial-intelligence software that is mapping where people live.[191] Facebook will use this map to identify areas where it can expand its Internet initiative.[192] One of the first twenty countries Facebook mapped was India.[193] As Facebook improves the detail and accuracy of its maps, it could begin mapping areas the Indian government doesn't want it to.

Google held a contest in India called Mapathon 2013. The objective was to have local residents map out their areas so Google could collect new information on the locations of hospitals, temples, and other buildings.

The contest succeeded. Google also ended up collecting data on secret Indian military bases, however, and published this information to the world.[194] The Indian government responded by saying Google had not obtained permission to map these areas.

When it comes to Facebook's artificial-intelligence maps, two challenges arise. First, Facebook could begin mapping areas it shouldn't, like Google did. Second, being software, Facebook's artificial intelligence could objectively map out India. It could identify areas based on poverty, socioeconomic factors, sanitation, disease, and more. This could paint a picture of India that doesn't sit well with New Delhi. The last time a technology company did this in India, it was banned.

The most famous action taken by the Indian government was in 1995, when it banned all sales of Windows 95.[195] Why? Of the 800,000 pixels that Microsoft had colored green to represent India, exactly eight pixels were a different shade of green to represent Kashmir, which India claims as its territory.[196] Microsoft had to recall 200,000 copies of Windows 95 and try to heal the "diplomatic wounds," all because the company painted a picture of India that didn't sit well with those in power.

Just as Microsoft ran into trouble over its artificial-intelligence chatbot, Tay, making insulting comments on Twitter,[197] so too could Facebook if it doesn't pay attention to this risk. Unlike SpaceKnow in China, Facebook is an extremely large company with a physical and digital footprint in India.

With 125 million users India represents Facebook's second biggest market as of 2016,[198] as well as its biggest market tomorrow.[199] Facebook's political relationship with India is already rocky, following a ban on Facebook's Free Basics, part of its Internet initiative.[200]

If the Indian government is not happy with how it is depicted in Facebook's maps, it could ask the company to change them. Facebook could reject this request, but it risks punishment from the Indian government — such as a ban. Monsanto faced this in India, with the Indian government saying Monsanto is welcome to leave the country if the company could not abide by the rules.

Once again, such a scenario risks involving the U.S. government, if Facebook were to demand the the ban be lifted or request other options besides implementing what the Indian government demands. Facebook needs India, but does India need Facebook?

Conclusion

As technology companies expand globally, the innovations they develop will lead them into unfamiliar territory. This culminates in a turning of the tables.

In the past, companies have been on the receiving end of the choices governments make. Now, governments are on the receiving end of the innovations companies sell.

This change will disrupt world affairs.

For governments, it'll mean a more reactive foreign policy. They'll be pulled into international disputes. For technology companies, it means every new product being created must be viewed from two perspectives: first, the benefits it creates, and second, the inherent risks it carries.

This changes the way the world operates. When a big data startup from Taiwan causes tensions in Bolivia, or an artificial-intelligence company from Australia fuels friction in Bangladesh, the manner in which geopolitical tensions emerge completely changes.

For decades, governments have directed world affairs. In the future, will it be technology companies?

CITATIONS

About Me

[1] The project was called "Explosive Times." It was a digital media project with an objective to research, analyze, and distill the most disruptive events changing the world, and then publish them on Twitter. It focused on world affairs, global economy, finance, social changes, and other topics.

[2] Abishur Prakash, "Forget the Markets, Robots Are China's New Worry," *Forbes*, January 28, 2016, www.forbes.com/sites/realspin/2016/01/28/forget-the-markets-robots-are-chinas-new-worry/#207d30fa1edb.

Meet the Historian

[3] Abishur Prakash, "Geopolitics Guides Military Robotics Race," *Robotics Business Review*, April 6, 2016, www.roboticsbusinessreview.com/geopolitics_guides_military_robotics_race.

[4] "Processing Power Compared," *Experts Exchange*, http://pages.experts-exchange.com/processing-power-compared.

[5] Peter Shadbolt, "FireChat in Hong Kong: How an app tapped its way into the protests," *CNN*, October 16, 2014, www.cnn.com/2014/10/16/tech/mobile/tomorrow-transformed-firechat.

[6] The "Next Machine Age" was originally coined by Aseem Prakash, founder of Karma Robotics, a robotics consultancy based out of North America. He used it to describe the next phase humanity and technology are

entering.

Chapter 1 - Embryonic Geopolitics

[7] National Institutes of Health, U.S. National Library of Medicine, "Fetal development," *Medline Plus*, September 26, 2015, www.nlm.nih.gov/medlineplus/ency/article/002398.htm.

[8] James A. O'Brien, "What Is The Difference Between An Embryo And A Fetus?" *The Bump*, www.thebump.com/a/difference-between-embryo-and-fetus.

[9] One of the technologies making this kind of editing possible is clustered regularly interspaced short palindromic repeats (CRISPR). CRISPR allows doctors to edit, cut, and replace certain parts of the DNA within the genome. It does this by deploying two molecules. The first is called Cas9, and is essentially a pair of scissors that can cut parts of the DNA at a determined location. The second molecule is RNA, which acts as a GPS system, guiding Cas9 to the right point in the DNA.

[10] Haroon Siddique, "British researchers get green light to genetically modify human embryos," *The Guardian*, February 1, 2016, www.theguardian.com/science/2016/feb/01/human-embryo-genetic-modify-regulator-green-light-research.

[11] Ewen Callaway, "UK scientists gain licence to edit genes in human embryos," *Nature* 530 (2016): 18, doi:10.1038/nature.2016.19270. www.nature.com/news/uk-scientists-gain-licence-to-edit-genes-in-human-embryos-1.19270

[12] Stephanie Linning, "Who said crime doesn't pay? Counting prostitution and drugs in the GDP figure has seen the UK's economy overtake France as fifth largest in the world," *Daily Mail*, December 27, 2014,

www.dailymail.co.uk/news/article-2888416/Who-said-crime-doesn-t-pay-Counting-prostitution-drugs-GDP-figure-seen-UK-s-economy-overtake-France-fifth-largest-world.html.

[13] "NHS charges for people from abroad," *Citizen's Advice*, www.citizensadvice.org.uk/healthcare/help-with-health-costs/nhs-charges-for-people-from-abroad.

[14] Tim Daiss, "International Court Rejects China's Claims To South China Sea," *Forbes*, July 12, 2016, www.forbes.com/sites/timdaiss/2016/07/12/philippines-wins-south-china-sea-case-against-china-court-issues-harsh-verdict/#27a247723a0a.

[15] In 2014, German universities became tuition-free. This free schooling can be accessed by any person in the world who wants to pursue post-secondary education in Germany.

[16] Dominic Bailey, Mick Ruddy, and Marina Shchukina, "Ageing China: Changes and challenges," *BBC News Asia*, September 20, 2012, www.bbc.com/news/world-asia-19630110.

[17] Morgan Winsor, "China's One-Child Policy Change Will Take Decades To Relieve Economic Pressures Of Aging Population, Experts Say," *International Business Times*, October 29, 2015, www.ibtimes.com/chinas-one-child-policy-change-will-take-decades-relieve-economic-pressures-aging-2161789.

[18] Aya Takada, "Japan's Next Generation of Farmers Could Be Robots," *Bloomberg*, April 22, 2016, www.bloomberg.com/news/articles/2016-04-23/robots-replacing-japan-s-farmers-seen-preserving-food-security.

[19] Adam Taylor, "It's official: Japan's population is dramatically shrinking," *The Washington Post*, February 26, 2016, www.washingtonpost.com/news/worldviews/wp/2016/02/26/its-official-japans-population-is-drastically-shrinking.

[20] Mariko Oi, "Who will look after Japan's elderly?" *BBC News*, March 16, 2015, www.bbc.com/news/world-asia-31901943.

[21] Associated Press, "Japan population to shrink by a third by 2060," *The Guardian*, January 30, 2012, www.theguardian.com/world/2012/jan/30/japan-population-shrink-third.

[22] Ian Sample, "Scientists genetically modify human embryos in controversial world first," *The Guardian*, April 23, 2015, www.theguardian.com/science/2015/apr/23/scientists-genetically-modify-human-embryos-in-controversial-world-first.

[23] Ewen Callaway, "Second Chinese team reports gene editing in human embryos," *Nature,* April 8, 2016, www.nature.com/news/second-chinese-team-reports-gene-editing-in-human-embryos-1.19718.

[24] "Netherlands to grown human embryos for research," *RT*, May 28, 2016, www.rt.com/news/344685-embryos-human-dutch-government.

Chapter 2 - Space Sovereignty

[25] Benjamin Lampkin, "10 Deep Facts About the Great Lakes," *Mental Floss*, February 1, 2016, http://mentalfloss.com/article/74674/10-deep-facts-about-great-lakes.

[26] Chris Matthews, "America Now Leads the World In This Surprising Category," *Fortune*, July 5, 2016, http://fortune.com/2016/07/05/oil-reserves-us.

[27] United Nations Office for Outer Space Affairs, "Treaty on Principles Governing the Activities of States in the Exploration and Use of Outer Space, including the Moon and Other Celestial Bodies," 1966,

www.unoosa.org/oosa/en/ourwork/spacelaw/treaties/intro
outerspacetreaty.html.

[28] James Vincent, "China wants to go to the dark side of the moon in 2018," *The Verge*, January 15, 2016, www.theverge.com/2016/1/15/10774508/china-dark-side-of-the-moon-2018.

[29] Ryan O'Hare, "China wants to land on Mars by 2021: Top official at the country's space agency reveals plans for mission to the red planet," *Daily Mail*, April 20, 2016, www.dailymail.co.uk/sciencetech/article-3549536/China-wants-land-Mars-2021-official-country-s-space-agency-reveals-plans-mission-red-planet.html.

[30] Ben Blanchard, "China to launch 'core module' for space station around 2018," *Reuters*, April 21, 2016, www.reuters.com/article/us-china-space-idUSKCN0XI07Y.

[31] Katherine Derla, "China To Launch Own Version of Hubble Telescope in 2020s," *Tech Times*, March 12, 2016, www.techtimes.com/articles/140536/20160312/china-to-launch-own-version-of-hubble-telescope-in-2020s.htm.

[32] Michael Martina, "China aims for manned moon landing by 2036,"*Reuters*, April 29, 2016, www.reuters.com/article/us-china-space-moon-idUSKCN0XQ0JT.

[33] Dann Berg, "China's manned space missions steadily working toward Mars," *The Verge*, July 10, 2013, www.theverge.com/2013/7/10/4510982/chinas-manned-space-missions-2040.

[34] This is a geopolitical theory, not an official strategy released by the Chinese Communist Party (CCP).

[35] Fabrizio Bozzato, "Moon Power: China's Pursuit of Lunar Helium-3," *The Diplomat*, June 16, 2014, http://thediplomat.com/2014/06/moon-power-chinas-pursuit-of-lunar-helium-3.

[36] John Hewitt, " China is going to mine the Moon for helium-3 fusion fuel," *Extreme Tech*, January 26, 2015, www.extremetech.com/extreme/197784-china-is-going-to-mine-the-moon-for-helium-3-fusion-fuel.

[37] Sarah Fecht, "Companies Can Now Officially Own Resources They Mine From Asteroids," *Popular Science*, November 30, 2015, http://www.popsci.com/companies-can-now-officially-own-resources-they-mine-from-asteroids.

[38] "'Platinum' asteroid potentially worth $5.4 trillion to pass Earth on Sunday," *RT*, July 18, 2015, https://www.rt.com/news/310170-platinum-asteroid-2011-uw-158/.

[39] "China launches world's 1st quantum satellite," *CBC*, August 16, 2016, www.cbc.ca/news/technology/china-quantum-satellite-1.3349383.

[40] Sarah Fecht, "Luxembourg Wants To Become Earth's Hub For Asteroid Mining," *Popular Science*, February 4, 2016, http://www.popsci.com/luxembourg-wants-to-become-gold-rush-town-for-space-mining.

[41] "Luxembourg sets aside 200 million euros to fund space mining ventures," *Reuters*, June 3, 2016, http://www.reuters.com/article/us-luxembourg-space-mining-idUSKCN0YP22H.

[42] "Robots May Start Moon Base Construction," *Solar System Exploration Research Virtual Institute*,

[43] Jennings Brown. "Pentagon Plans To Send Giant Robotic Arms Into Space," *Vocativ*, July 26, 2016, www.vocativ.com/343595/space-robotic-arms.

[44] Jelor Gallego. "New Tech Installed on The ISS Set To Form Solar System-Wide 'Internet'," *Futurism*, June 26, 2016, http://futurism.com/new-tech-installed-on-the-iss-set-to-form-solar-system-wide-internet.

[45] Jonathan Amos, "Why India's Mars mission is so cheap - and thrilling," *BBC*, September 24, 2014, www.bbc.com/news/science-environment-29341850.

[46] "After success with Mars, ISRO is now planning a mission to Venus," *Defence Update,* December 26, 2015, http://defenceupdate.in/after-success-with-mars-isro-is-now-planning-a-mission-to-venus/.

[47] "India plans to launch 60 space missions in 5 years," *Space Daily*, February 23, 2016, http://www.spacedaily.com/reports/India_plans_to_launch_60_space_missions_in_5_years_999.html.

[48] 'ISRO Crosses 50 International Customer Satellite Launch Mark," *Indian Space Research Organisation,* http://www.isro.gov.in/isro-crosses-50-international-customer-satellite-launch-mark.

[49] Song Ji-sun, "Korea's space programs enters next phase KSLV-2," *Arirang*, April 18, 2013, http://www.arirang.com/News/News_View.asp?nseq=146155.

[50] "Japan aims for Moon base by 2030," *New Scientist*, August 2, 2006, https://www.newscientist.com/article/dn9658-japan-aims-for-moon-base-by-2030/.

[51] "Spray-painting robot makes painters redundant," *Global Construction Review,* October 27, 2016, http://www.globalconstructionreview.com/innovation/spray-painting-robot-mak7es-painte7rs-redund7ant/.

[52] Jason Torchinsky, "Russia Reportedly Plans To Build A Lunar Base By The 2030s," *Jalopnik*, December 1, 2015, http://jalopnik.com/russia-reportedly-plans-to-build-a-lunar-base-by-the-20-1745479179.

[53] Kieron Monks, "Nigeria plans to send an astronaut to space by 2030," *CNN*, April 6, 2016, http://www.cnn.com/2016/04/06/africa/nigeria-nasrda-space-astronaut.

Chapter 3 - Dangerous Automation

[54] Centers for Disease Control and Prevention, "A Robot May Not Injure a Worker: Working safely with robots," November 20, 2015, http://blogs.cdc.gov/niosh-science-blog/2015/11/20/working-with-robots/.

[55] An example of a modern-day service robot is the Roomba robotic vacuum cleaner from iRobot, which can vacuum floors, navigate environments, and pick up dirt on its own — without human input.

[56] Abishur Prakash, "Why Robot Law Around Industrial Automation Varies Worldwide," *Robotics Business Review*, May 11, 2016, www.roboticsbusinessreview.com/why-robot-law-around-industrial-automation-varies-worldwide/.

[57] World Bank, "Labour force, total," http://data.worldbank.org/indicator/SL.TLF.TOTL.IN.

[58] Emiko Jozuka, "Robots Could Take Over Nearly 50 Percent of Jobs in Japan in the Next 20 Years," *Vice*, December 3, 2015, http://motherboard.vice.com/read/robots-could-take-over-nearly-50-percent-of-jobs-in-japan-in-the-next-20-years.

[59] Their calculations were broken down into 80 million jobs in the United States and 15 million jobs in the United Kingdom.

[60] Chris Smith, "Bank of England: 95 million jobs going to robots in the next 10 to 20 years," *BGR,* November 16, 2015, http://bgr.com/2015/11/16/robots-replacing-human-jobs/.

[61]"Five Million Jobs by 2020: the Real Challenge of the Fourth Industrial Revolution," *World Economic Forum*, January 18, 2016, www.weforum.org/press/2016/01/five-million-jobs-by-2020-the-real-challenge-of-the-fourth-industrial-revolution/.

[62] Erik Brynjolfsson and Andrew Mcafee, "Why Workers Are Losing the War Against Machines," *The Atlantic*, October 26, 2011, www.theatlantic.com/business/archive/2011/10/why-

workers-are-losing-the-war-against-machines/247278.

[63] Paul A. Eisenstein, "Is Your (Auto) Job About to be Automated," *The Detroit Bureau*, March 13, 2015, www.thedetroitbureau.com/2015/03/is-your-auto-job-about-to-be-automated.

[64] Daniel Boffey, "Dutch city plans to pay citizens a 'basic income', and Greens say it could work in the UK," *The Guardian*, December 26, 2015, www.theguardian.com/world/2015/dec/26/dutch-city-utrecht-basic-income-uk-greens.

[65] Philip Oltermann, "State handouts for all? Europe set to pilot universal basic incomes," *The Guardian*, June 2, 2016, www.theguardian.com/world/2016/jun/02/state-handouts-for-all-europe-set-to-pilot-universal-basic-incomes.

[66] Keith Leslie, "Ontario's Basic Income Experiment Coming This Fall," *Huffington Post*, March 13, 2016, www.huffingtonpost.ca/2016/03/13/ontario-will-test-idea-of-a-guaranteed-minimum-income-to-ease-poverty_n_9451076.html.

[67] "Switzerland's voters reject basic income plan," *BBC*, June 5, 2016, www.bbc.com/news/world-europe-36454060.

[68] "Technology At Work v2.0," *Oxford Martin*, January, 2016, http://www.oxfordmartin.ox.ac.uk/downloads/reports/Citi_GPS_Technology_Work_2.pdf.

[69] "Policy Basics: Where Do Federal Tax Revenues Come From?," *Center on Budget and Policy Priorities*, March 4, 2016, http://www.cbpp.org/research/policy-basics-where-do-federal-tax-revenues-come-from.

[70] Jeff Desjardins, "$60 Trillion of World Debt in One Visualization," *Visual Capitalist*, August 6, 2015, http://www.visualcapitalist.com/60-trillion-of-world-debt-in-one-visualization/.

[71] "Global GDP (gross domestic product) at current prices

from 2010 to 2020 (in billion U.S. dollars)," *Statista,* https://www.statista.com/statistics/268750/global-gross-domestic-product-gdp/.

[72] Elaine Moore, "Belgium issues 100-year bond in private sale," *Financial Times*, April 26, 2016, https://www.ft.com/content/bc6f3e00-0ba7-11e6-9456-444ab5211a2f.

[73] If bonds are the way to go, for Canada, the government could release a bond tied to freshwater — considering Canada has one of the largest freshwater reserves in the world. The government could sell a bond tied to the value of freshwater, which is only set to rise in the future.

[74] The concept of a "productivity tax" was originally proposed by Aseem Prakash, the founder of Karma Robotics, a robotics consultancy based in North America.

[75] Jörn Poltz, "Adidas to return mass shoe production to Germany in 2017," *Reuters*, May 25, 2016, http://uk.reuters.com/article/uk-adidas-manufacturing-idUKKCN0YF1YE.

[76] *Jörg Luyken,* "Are robots about to take away 18 million jobs?," *The Local,* May 4, 2015, http://www.thelocal.de/20150504/are-robots-about-to-take-away-18-million-jobs.

[77] Such countries could be called "automation havens," like the tax havens of today.

[78] Abishur Prakash, "Why Robot Law Around Industrial Automation Varies Worldwide," *Robotics Business Review*, May 11, 2016, https://www.roboticsbusinessreview.com/why_robot_law_around_industrial_automation_varies_worldwide/.

[79] Abishur Prakash, "Four Ways Robotics Is Changing Countries," *Medium*, May 3, 2016, medium.com/next-geopolitics/four-ways-robotics-is-changing-countries-2a7ccc9a8d4d#.yh64lvvxj.

[80] Maria Sheahan, "China seeks top-10 automation ranking by 2020: robot industry group," *Reuters*, July 22,

2016, www.reuters.com/article/us-china-robots-forecast-idUSKCN102104.

[81] Benjamin Kang Lim, Matthew Miller and David Stanway, "Exclusive: China to lay off five to six million workers, earmarks at least $23 billion," *Reuters*, March 3, 2016, http://www.reuters.com/article/us-china-economy-layoffs-exclusive-idUSKCN0W33DS.

[82] Mark Magnier, "China's Economic Growth in 2015 Is Slowest in 25 Years," *The Wall Street Journal*, January 19, 2016, http://www.wsj.com/articles/china-economic-growth-slows-to-6-9-on-year-in-2015-1453169398.

[83] Javier C. Hernandez, "China Censors WeChat Rumors, Including the One About Robots Taking Over," *The New York Times*, June 24, 2016, http://www.nytimes.com/2016/06/25/world/what-in-the-world/china-wechat-censor-rumors.html?_r=1.

[84] This was an idea proposed by Patrick Perlmutter, the founder of a UX design company called Y-Hat.

[85] Ben Hirschler, "Robots, new working ways to cost five million jobs by 2020, Davos study says," *Reuters*, January 18, 2016, http://www.reuters.com/article/us-davos-meeting-employment-idUSKCN0UW0NV.

[86] Georgina Prodhan, "Europe's robots to become "electronic persons" under draft plan," *Reuters*, June 21, 2016, http://in.reuters.com/article/europe-robotics-lawmaking-idINKCN0Z72CW.

Chapter 4 - Food Cloning

[87] "Some 3.2 billion people now online, but number still falls short of Internet target – UN report," *UN News Centre*, November 30, 2015, http://www.un.org/apps/news/story.asp?NewsID=52690#.V2FqquYrJE4.

[88] "Global economy will double to $72 trillion in 25

years: World Bank," *Indian Express*, December 16, 2006, http://archive.indianexpress.com/news/global-economy-will-double-to--72-trillion-in-25-years-world-bank-/18652/.

[89] New Zealand Foreign Affairs & Trade, "Regional Comprehensive Economic Partnership (RCEP)," https://www.mfat.govt.nz/en/trade/free-trade-agreements/agreements-under-negotiation/rcep/.

[90] In the future, if cloned individuals need a replacement organ like a liver, kidney, or lung, they could tap their clone.

[91] Samantha Grossman, "These Maps Show Every Country's Most Valuable Exports," *TIME*, May 21, 2014, http://time.com/106666/world-export-maps/.

[92] Rob Cook, "World Beef Exports: Ranking Of Countries," *Beef2Live*, November 9, 2016, http://beef2live.com/story-world-beef-exports-ranking-countries-0-106903.

[93] PK Krishnakumar, "We can't kill cows, but globally lead in beef exports," *The Economic Times,* April 23, 2015, http://economictimes.indiatimes.com/news/economy/foreign-trade/we-cant-kill-cows-but-globally-lead-in-beef-exports/articleshow/47020416.cms.

[94] Brian Wang, "Boyalife CEO plans to clones Woolly Mammoths and possibly humans after getting cloning factory scaled to million cows per year by 2020," *Next Big Future*, December 2, 2015, http://www.nextbigfuture.com/2015/12/boyalife-ceo-plans-to-clones-woolly.html.

[95] Alexandra Ossola, "Chinese Factory Will Make Cloned Beef on A Massive Scale," *Popular Science*, November 30, 2015, http://www.popsci.com/chinese-company-will-make-cloned-beef-on-massive-scale.

[96] "Factory In China To Produce 1 Million Cloned Cows By 2020, Says It Has The Technology To Clone

Humans," *Malaysia Digest*, December 3, 2015,
http://malaysiandigest.com/features/582441-factory-in-
china-to-produce-1-million-cloned-cows-by-2020-says-it-
has-the-technology-to-clone-humans.html.

[97] "Consumption Facts," *Real Coffee*,
http://www.realcoffee.co.uk/coffee-
encyclopedia/trivia/consumption-facts/.

[98] "Coffee producing countries," *European Coffee
Federation*, http://www.ecf-coffee.org/about-
coffee/coffee-facts.

[99] Simran Kholsa, "This map shows which export makes
your country the most money," *PRI*, May 14, 2014,
http://www.pri.org/stories/2014-05-14/map-shows-which-
export-makes-your-country-most-money.

[100] Julie Craves, "Nestlè distributes mass-produced
robusta clones," *Coffee Habitat*, June 24, 2008,
http://www.coffeehabitat.com/2008/06/nestle-distributes-
mass-produced-robusta-clones/.

[101] "DA tests Nestlè's coffee clones," *Rappler*, March 6,
2012, http://www.rappler.com/business/2157-da-tests-
nestl%C3%A8-s-coffee-clones.

[102] Peter Imbong, "Philippines tries to reignite
production," *Nikkei Asian Review*, December 18, 2014,
http://asia.nikkei.com/Politics-
Economy/Economy/Philippines-tries-to-reignite-
production?page=2.

[103] World Trade Organization, "Standards committee
discusses tyres, toy safety and food," *November 4-6,
2015,
https://www.wto.org/english/news_e/news15_e/tbt_10nov
15_e.htm.*

Chapter 5 - New Rules of War

[104] Abishur Prakash, "Geopolitics Guides Military

Robotics Race," *Robotics Business Review*, April 6, 2016, www.roboticsbusinessreview.com/geopolitics_guides_mil itary_robotics_race.

[105] Nafeez Ahmed, "The Pentagon is building a 'self-aware' killer robot army fueled by social media," Medium, May 12, 2016, https://medium.com/insurge-intelligence/the-pentagon-is-building-a-self-aware-killer-robot-army-fueled-by-social-media-bd1b55944298#.fgbenk21m.

[106] Sarah Knapton, "Killer robots will leave humans 'utterly defenceless' warns professor," *The Telegraph*, May 27, 2015, http://www.telegraph.co.uk/news/science/science-news/11633838/Killer-robots-will-leave-humans-utterly-defenceless-warns-professor.html.

[107] Jack Crosbie, "DARPA Releases Photo of "Sea Hunter" Self-Driving Drone Ship on Maiden Voyage," Inverse, June 10, 2016, https://www.inverse.com/article/16840-darpa-releases-photo-of-sea-hunter-self-driving-drone-ship-on-maiden-voyage.

[108] Ruth Reader, "DARPA's Autonomous Armored Vehicle Can Dodge Bombs and Rockets by Itself," *Mic*, April 28, 2016, https://mic.com/articles/142087/darpa-s-autonomous-armored-vehicle-can-dodge-bombs-and-rockets-by-itself#.TF1EMSIPi.

[109] David Hambling, "Russia Wants Autonomous Fighting Robots, and Lots of Them," *Popular Mechanics*, May 12, 2014, http://www.popularmechanics.com/military/a10511/russia-wants-autonomous-fighting-robots-and-lots-of-them-16787165/.

[110] Pat Medina, "Russia experiments with autonomous military robot squadrons," *Futurism*, October 20, 2015, http://futurism.com/russia-experiments-with-autonomous-military-robot-squadrons/.

[111] Jeffrey Lin and P.W. Singer, "The Great Underwater Wall of Robots: Chinese Exhibit Shows Off Sea Drones," *Popular Science*, June 22, 2016, http://www.popsci.com/great-underwater-wall-robots-chinese-exhibit-shows-off-sea-drones.

[112] Jeffrey Lin and P.W. Singer, "China Debuts Anbot, The Police Robot," *Popular Science*, April 27, 2016, http://www.popsci.com/china-debuts-anbot-police-robot.

[113] Patrick Tucker, "The Pentagon is Nervous about Russian and Chinese Killer Robots," *Defense One*, December 14, 2015, http://www.defenseone.com/threats/2015/12/pentagon-nervous-about-russian-and-chinese-killer-robots/124465/?oref=DefenseOneFB&&&.

[114] Abishur Prakash, "Geopolitics Guides Military Robotics Race," *Robotics Business Review*, April 6, 2016, www.roboticsbusinessreview.com/geopolitics_guides_military_robotics_race.

[115] Kelsey D. Atherton, "The U.S. Military Is Patrolling Djibouti With Robot Golf Carts," *Popular Science*, July 26, 2016, http://www.popsci.com/american-military-patrols-djibouti-with-robot-golfcarts.

[116] Abishur Prakash, "Geopolitics Guides Military Robotics Race," *Robotics Business Review*, April 6, 2016, www.roboticsbusinessreview.com/geopolitics_guides_military_robotics_race.

[117] "Diplomats discuss laws for autonomous military weapons," *Business Insider,* April 20, 2016, http://www.businessinsider.com/diplomats-discuss-laws-for-autonomous-military-weapons-2016-4.

[118] "Japan pushes for basic AI rules at G-7 tech meeting," *The Japan Times*, April 29, 2016, http://www.japantimes.co.jp/news/2016/04/29/national/japan-pushes-basic-ai-rules-g-7-tech-meeting.

[119] James Eng, "OPM Hack: Government Finally Starts Notifying 21.5 Million Victims," *NBC News*, October 1,

2015, http://www.nbcnews.com/tech/security/opm-hack-government-finally-starts-notifying-21-5-million-victims-n437126.

[120] Ellen Nakashima, "Chinese government has arrested hackers it says breached OPM database," *The Washington Post*, December 2, 2015, www.washingtonpost.com/world/national-security/chinese-government-has-arrested-hackers-suspected-of-breaching-opm-database/2015/12/02/0295b918-990c-11e5-8917-653b65c809eb_story.html.

[121] Jonathan Chew, "China Says It Wasn't Behind the Massive U.S. Government Hack," *Fortune*, December 2, 2015, http://fortune.com/2015/12/02/china-opm-hack/.

[122] Sean Gallagher, "China and Russia cross-referencing OPM data, other hacks to out US spies," *Ars Technica*, August 31, 2015, http://arstechnica.com/security/2015/08/china-and-russia-cross-referencing-opm-data-other-hacks-to-out-us-spies/.

[123] Kay Armin Serjoie, "Iran Investigates If Series of Oil Industry Accidents Were Caused by Cyber Attack," *TIME*, August 12, 2016, http://time.com/4450433/iran-investigates-if-series-of-oil-industry-accidents-were-caused-by-cyber-attack/.

[124] Joseph Berger, "A Dam, Small and Unsung, Is Caught Up in an Iranian Hacking Case," *The New York Times*, March 25, 2016, http://www.nytimes.com/2016/03/26/nyregion/rye-brook-dam-caught-in-computer-hacking-case.html?_r=0.

[125] Hal Hodson and Sally Adee, "Autonomous AI guards to stalk the internet fighting hackers," *New Scientist*, August 17, 2016, https://www.newscientist.com/article/mg23130870-900-autonomous-ai-guards-to-stalk-the-internet-fighting-hackers.

[126] Stuxnet was a computer virus allegedly developed by

the US and Israel to halt Iran's nuclear program. Unlike traditional viruses that only affect software, Stuxnet also damaged physical infrastructure that was integral to Iran's nuclear program — centrifuges.

[127] Robert Lemos, "Hackers Infiltrated Ukrainian Power Grid Months Before Cyber-Attack," *eWeek,* March 23, 2016, http://www.eweek.com/security/hackers-infiltrated-ukrainian-power-grid-months-before-cyber-attack.html.

[128] "Russia 'was behind German parliament hack'," *BBC*, May 13, 2016, http://www.bbc.com/news/technology-36284447.

[129] Andrea Shalal, "Massive cyber attack could trigger NATO response: Stoltenberg," *Reuters*, June 16, 2016, http://www.reuters.com/article/us-cyber-nato-idUSKCN0Z12NE.

[130] "Combat robots to protect Russian oil and gas infrastructure in Arctic - Foundation," *Interfax*, October 21, 2014, http://www.interfax.com/newsinf.asp?id=545385.

[131] "Here's how India plans to completely 'lock' the border with Pakistan," *DNA*, April 11, 2016, http://www.dnaindia.com/india/report-here-s-how-centre-plans-to-completely-lock-border-with-pakistan-2200664.

Chapter 6 - Technological Terrorism

[132] Mark Harris, "FBI Warns driverless cars could be used as 'lethal weapons'," *The Guardian*, July 16, 2014, www.theguardian.com/technology/2014/jul/16/google-fbi-driverless-cars-leathal-weapons-autonomous.

[133] Pete Bigelow, "ISIS could use a self-driving car to deliver a bomb," *Autoblog*, March 15, 2016, http://www.autoblog.com/2016/03/15/isis-terrorists-bomb-self-driving-cars-sxsw/.

[134] Sam Blum, "ISIS Technicians Work on Self-Driving

Cars at Terrorism R&D Lab in Leaked Video," *Inverse*, January 7, 2016, https://www.inverse.com/article/9974-isis-technicians-work-on-self-driving-cars-at-terrorism-r-d-lab-in-leaked-video.

[135] Andy Greenberg, "Hackers Remotely Kill A Jeep On The Highway - With Me In It," *WIRED*, July 21, 2015, www.wired.com/2015/07/hackers-remotely-kill-jeep-highway.

[136] To protect people, the government could request that automakers open up to authorities large quantities of data that provide information on where people are driving, when they are driving, and more. Would this be considered an invasion of privacy? Is there an alternative?

[137] Tom Brooks-Pollock, "Drones 'could be used as flying bombs for terror attack on passenger jet'," *The Telegraph,* December 12, 2014, http://www.telegraph.co.uk/news/uknews/terrorism-in-the-uk/11290086/Drones-could-be-used-as-flying-bombs-for-terror-attack-on-passenger-jet.html.

[138] Tom Brooks-Pollock, "Drone was 'within 20ft' of crashing into passenger plane landing at Heathrow," *The Telegraph*, December 12, 2014, http://www.telegraph.co.uk/news/aviation/11289406/Drone-was-within-20ft-of-crashing-into-passenger-plane-landing-at-Heathrow.html.

[139] Leo Kelion, "DJI drones gain geo-fencing safety feature opt-out," *BBC*, July 5, 2016, http://www.bbc.com/news/technology-36717538.

[140] Nick Lavars, "US airports to put drone-disabling system to the test," *New Atlas*, June 1, 2016, http://newatlas.com/us-radio-beams-airports/43617/.

[141] Evan Ackerman, "Dutch Police Training Eagles to Take Down Drones," *IEEE Spectrum*, February 1, 2016, http://spectrum.ieee.org/automaton/robotics/drones/dutch-police-training-eagles-to-take-down-drones.

[142] Stacey Klein, "Drone Buzzes President Barack

Obama's Motorcade in Hawaii," *NBC News,* December 29, 2015, http://www.nbcnews.com/news/us-news/drone-buzzes-president-barack-obama-s-motorcade-hawaii-n487176.

[143] Matthew Weaver, "UK should prepare for use of drones in terrorist attacks, says thinktank," *The Guardian*, January 11, 2016, https://www.theguardian.com/uk-news/2016/jan/11/drones-terrorist-attacks-security-thinktank.

[144] Jason Dearen, "Drones fly controlled by nothing more than people's thoughts," *Independent*, April 22, 2016, http://www.independent.co.uk/news/science/drones-brain-thoughts-controlled-bci-brain-computer-interface-brain-controlled-interface-a6996781.html.

[145] Jon Fingas, "GE's smart appliances let you take control with your phone," *Engadget*, January 5, 2015, www.engadget.com/2015/01/05/ge-profile-smart-appliances.

[146] Darlene Storm, "Black Hat: Nest thermostat turned into a smart spy in 15 seconds," *Computerworld*, August 11, 2014, http://www.computerworld.com/article/2476599/cybercrime-hacking/black-hat-nest-thermostat-turned-into-a-smart-spy-in-15-seconds.html.

[147] Amy Nordrum, "Popular Internet of Things Forecast of 50 Billion Devices by 2020 Is Outdated," *IEEE Spectrum,* August 18, 2016, http://spectrum.ieee.org/tech-talk/telecom/internet/popular-internet-of-things-forecast-of-50-billion-devices-by-2020-is-outdated.

Chapter 7 - Drone Dependency

[148] "Parrot Bebop 2," *Parrot,* www.parrot.com/usa/products/bebop2.

[149] Jonathan Vanian, "GE is using drones to inspect the

power grid," *Fortune*, October 23, 2015,
http://fortune.com/2015/10/23/ge-drones-power-grid/.
[150] Jessi Hempel, "Inside Facebook's Ambitious Plan To
Connect The Whole World," *WIRED*, January 19, 2016,
www.wired.com/2016/01/facebook-zuckerberg-internet-
org.
[151] Lily Kuo, "Drone delivery could give Africa's HIV-
positive babies a fighting chance at survival," *Quartz
Africa*, March 15, 2016, http://qz.com/639417/drone-
delivery-could-give-africas-hiv-positive-babies-a-better-
chance-at-survival/.
[152] "Crime-fighting drones for the City of Cape Town,"
My Broadband, May 11, 2015,
http://mybroadband.co.za/news/gadgets/125794-crime-
fighting-drones-for-the-city-of-cape-town.html.
[153] Gitonga Njeru, "Kenya to deploy drones in all national
parks in bid to tackle poaching," *The Guardian*, April 25,
2014,
https://www.theguardian.com/environment/2014/apr/25/k
enya-drones-national-parks-poaching.
[154] "Rwanda chosen for world's first 'drone-port' to deliver
medical supplies," *The Guardian*, September 30, 2015,
https://www.theguardian.com/technology/2015/sep/30/rw
anda-chosen-for-worlds-first-drone-port-to-deliver-
medical-supplies.
[155] "Rwandan Government Signs MoU for Drone
Delivery of Blood Supplies to Remote Areas," *African
Defense*, February 12, 2016, http://www.african-
defense.com/defense-news/rwandan-government-signs-
mou-for-drone-delivery-of-blood-supplies-to-remote-
areas/.
[156] Grace Schneider, "UPS will spend $800k on drone
project in Africa," *Courier-Journal*, May 11, 2016,
http://www.courier-
journal.com/story/money/companies/2016/05/10/ups-
spend-800k-drone-project-africa/84195482/.

[157] "Rwanda - Infrastructure, power, and communications," *Nations Encyclopedia*, http://www.nationsencyclopedia.com/economies/Africa/Rwanda-INFRASTRUCTURE-POWER-AND-COMMUNICATIONS.html.
[158] "Country Profile - Rwanda," *Feed The Future*, https://www.feedthefuture.gov/country/rwanda.
[159] Francesco Femia and Caitlin Werrell, "Syria: Climate Change, Drought and Social Unrest," *The Center for Climate & Security*, February 29, 2012, https://climateandsecurity.org/2012/02/29/syria-climate-change-drought-and-social-unrest/.
[160] "India caste unrest: Ten million without water in Delhi," *BBC*, February 22, 2016, http://www.bbc.com/news/world-asia-india-35627819.

Chapter 8 - Predictive Foreign Policy

[161] Merriam-Webster, "artificial intelligence," www.merriam-webster.com/dictionary/artificial%20intelligence.
[162] "Every Day Big Data Statistics - 2.5 Quintillion Bytes Of Data Created Daily," *VCloud News*, April 5, 2015, http://www.vcloudnews.com/every-day-big-data-statistics-2-5-quintillion-bytes-of-data-created-daily/.
[163] Shea Bennett, "What Happens Online In 60 Seconds? Incredible Statistics, Facts & Figures! [INFOGRAPHIC]," *Adweek*, July 25, 2013, http://www.adweek.com/socialtimes/online-60-seconds/488297.
[164] "Artificial intelligence to analyze ethnic relations in Russia," *Russia Beyond The Headlines*, January 24, 2016, http://rbth.com/news/2016/01/24/artificial-intelligence-to-analyze-ethnic-relations-in-russia_561879.
[165] "Baidu develops AI algorithm to predict crowds, avoid

stampedes," *ChinaDaily USA*, March 25, 2016, http://usa.chinadaily.com.cn/china/2016-03/25/content_24093630.htm.

[166] Mayank Bhardwaj, "India's colonial-era monsoon forecasting to get high-tech makeover," *Reuters,* June 9, 2016, http://in.reuters.com/article/india-monsoon-forecasting-idINKCN0YT2RQ.

[167] Alec Luhn, "Russia signs 30-year deal worth $400bn to deliver gas to China," *The Guardian,* May 21, 2014, https://www.theguardian.com/world/2014/may/21/russia-30-year-400bn-gas-deal-china.

[168] James Paton and Aibing Guo, "Russia, China Add to $400 Billion Gas Deal With Accord," *Bloomberg*, November 9, 2014, http://www.bloomberg.com/news/articles/2014-11-10/russia-china-add-to-400-billion-gas-deal-with-accord.

[169] Ankit Panda, "A First: Chinese Naval Vessel Enters Senkaku Contiguous Zone in East China Sea," *The Diplomat*, June 9, 2016, http://thediplomat.com/2016/06/a-first-chinese-naval-vessel-enters-senkaku-contiguous-zone-in-east-china-sea/.

[170] Abishur Prakash, "AI Competition Seen as Key to National Security," *Robotics Business Review,* April 12, 2016, https://www.roboticsbusinessreview.com/ai_competition_seen_as_key_to_national_security/.

[171] Dave Majumdar, "Revealed: Pentagon's Plan to Defeat Russian and Chinese Radar With A.I.," *The National Interest*, February 29, 2016, http://nationalinterest.org/blog/the-buzz/revealed-pentagons-plan-defeat-russian-chinese-radar-ai-15357.

[172] Tyler MacDonald, "DARPA: Neural Implant Will Give Drones Human-Like Artificial Intelligence," *HNGN*, February 10, 2016, http://www.hngn.com/articles/177915/20160210/darpa-neural-implant-will-give-drones-human-artificial-

intelligence.htm.

[173] Philip Iglauer, "South Korea promises $3b for AI R&D after AlphaGo 'shock'," *ZDNet*, March 22, 2016, http://www.zdnet.com/article/south-korea-promises-3b-for-ai-r-d-after-alphago-shock/.

[174] Abishur Prakash, "AI Competition Seen as Key to National Security," *Robotics Business Review,* April 12, 2016, https://www.roboticsbusinessreview.com/ai_competition_seen_as_key_to_national_security/.

[175] "India overtakes China as top FDI destination: Report," *Business Standard*, April 22, 2016, http://www.business-standard.com/article/economy-policy/india-overtakes-china-as-top-fdi-destination-report-116042200192_1.html.

[176] Cade Metz, "The Rise Of The Artificially Intelligent Hedge Fund," *WIRED*, January 25, 2016, https://www.wired.com/2016/01/the-rise-of-the-artificially-intelligent-hedge-fund.

[177] Tom Redmond and Toshiro Hasegawa, "This Japanese Robot Calls the Market Better Than a Human," *Bloomberg*, February 17, 2016, https://www.bloomberg.com/news/articles/2016-02-17/the-japanese-quant-who-made-a-robot-for-calling-the-stock-market.

[178] Guy Chazan, "Berlin and Brussels wary of Chinese robotics bid," *Financial Times*, June 13, 2016, https://www.ft.com/content/acbda1cc-3186-11e6-bda0-04585c31b153.

[179] Vivek Wadhwa, "The amazing artificial intelligence we were promised is coming, finally," *The Washington Post*, June 17, 2016, https://www.washingtonpost.com/news/innovations/wp/2016/06/17/the-amazing-artificial-intelligence-we-were-promised-is-coming-finally/.

[180] Dan Patterson, "United Nations CITO: Artificial

Intelligence will be humanity's final innovation," *TechRepublic,* February 23, 2016, http://www.techrepublic.com/article/united-nations-cito/.

[181] This is essentially "turning the tables." In the past, humans told technology what to do. Going forward, with artificial intelligence, technology could tell humans what to do. This proposition isn't based on the idea that technology will become our overlord. Instead, much of the thinking and analysis that humans once had to do would be completed by artificial intelligence. We would just follow the instructions we'd been forced to create in the past.

Bonus Chapter - Robotic Soft Power

[182] "Russia grants $200 million loan to Armenia for purchasing weapons," *Russia Beyond The Headlines,* February 19, 2016, http://rbth.com/defence/2016/02/19/russia-grants-200-million-loan-to-armenia-for-purchasing-weapons_569219.

[183] Will Knight, "A Popular Chinese Virtual Assistant Is Ready to Control Millions of Robots," *MIT Technology Review*, June 14, 2016, https://www.technologyreview.com/s/601539/a-popular-chinese-virtual-assistant-is-ready-to-control-millions-of-robots/.

Bonus Chapter - Business Induced Geopolitics

[184] James Stafford, "War Between Saudi Arabia and Iran Could Send Oil Prices To $250," *OilPrice*, January 12, 2016, http://oilprice.com/Energy/Oil-Prices/War-Between-Saudi-Arabia-And-Iran-Could-Send-Oil-Prices-

To-250.html.

[185] Sophie McNeill, "Saudi Arabia severs ties with Iran over reaction to execution of Shiite cleric Nimr al-Nimr," *ABC*, January 4, 2016, http://www.abc.net.au/news/2016-01-04/saudi-arabia-severs-ties-with-iran/7065624.

[186] "ISM Manufacturing Index," *Investopedia*, www.investopedia.com/terms/i/ism-mfg.asp.

[187] "Hedge Funds Look to Space With New China Economy Gauge," *Bloomberg*, March 13, 2016, http://www.bloomberg.com/news/articles/2016-03-13/hedge-funds-look-to-space-with-new-china-economy-gauge.

[188] Paul Carsten, "China bans use of Microsoft's Windows 8 on government computers," *Reuters*, May 20, 2014, http://www.reuters.com/article/us-microsoft-china-idUSBREA4J07Q20140520.

[189] Gordon G. Chang, "China Cuts Off McKinsey, Other U.S. Consultants To Retaliate Against Cyber Indictments," *Forbes*, May 25, 2014, http://www.forbes.com/sites/gordonchang/2014/05/25/china-cuts-off-mckinsey-other-u-s-consultants-to-retaliate-against-cyber-indictments/#6c9036e26232.

[190] Richi Jennings, "IBM banned from China banks in 'trial'," *Computerworld*, May 28, 2014, http://www.computerworld.com/article/2476349/network-servers/ibm-banned-from-china-banks-in--trial-.html.

[191] Nick Statt, "Facebook is using AI to make detailed maps of where people live," *The Verge*, February 22, 2016, http://www.theverge.com/2016/2/22/11075456/facebook-population-density-maps-internet-org.

[192] "Connecting the world," *Internet.org,* https://info.internet.org/en/

[193] "Facebook's AI team maps Earth to beam internet access to all," *Hindustan Times*, March 14, 2016, http://www.hindustantimes.com/tech/facebook-s-ai-team-

maps-earth-to-beam-internet-access-to-all/story-CmyknDmrV7Qut2qdzTWATJ.html.

[194] Kelsey D. Atherton, "How Google's Mapathon May Have Compromised India's National Security," *Popular Science*, July 29, 2014, http://www.popsci.com/article/technology/india-investigates-google-mapping-project.

[195] "Win 95 banned in India due to timezone map," *ICANN*, August 30, 2001, https://mm.icann.org/pipermail/tz/1995-August/009390.html.

[196] Jo Best, "How eight pixels cost Microsoft millions," *CNET*, April 19, 2004, https://www.cnet.com/news/how-eight-pixels-cost-microsoft-millions/.

[197] James Vincent, "Twitter taught Microsoft's AI chatbot to be a racist asshole in less than a day," *The Verge*, March 24, 2016, http://www.theverge.com/2016/3/24/11297050/tay-microsoft-chatbot-racist.

[198] "Facebook user base has now climbed to 125 million users in India," *Firstpost*, June 29, 2015, http://tech.firstpost.com/news-analysis/facebook-user-base-has-now-climbed-to-125-million-users-in-india-272186.html.

[199] "Facebook to Have Largest Users from India by 2017: Study," *The New Indian Express*, January 22, 2015, http://www.newindianexpress.com/nation/2015/jan/22/Facebook-to-Have-Largest-Users-from-India-by-2017-Study-708391.html.

[200] James Vincent, "Facebook's Free Basics service has been banned in India," *The Verge*, February 8, 2016, http://www.theverge.com/2016/2/8/10913398/free-basics-india-regulator-ruling.

www.ingramcontent.com/pod-product-compliance
Lightning Source LLC
Chambersburg PA
CBHW072238270326
41930CB00010B/2180